# I Almost Divorced My Husband But I Went
# ON STRIKE INSTEAD

# Sherri Mills

## I Almost Divorced My Husband But I Went
# ON STRIKE INSTEAD

BONNEVILLE BOOKS
SPRINGVILLE, UTAH

Dedicated to my wonderful husband, Gerald.

ISBN 13: 978-1-59955-517-1

Published by Bonneville Books, an imprint of Cedar Fort, Inc., 2373 W. 700 S., Springville, UT 84663
Distributed by Cedar Fort, Inc., www.cedarfort.com

LIBRARY OF CONGRESS CATALOGING-IN-PUBLICATION DATA

Mills, Sherri (Sherri M.), 1941-
  I almost divorced my husband, but I went on strike instead / Sherri Mills.
    p. cm.
  Summary: A step-by-step plan to redistribute domestic responsibilities and
ultimately avoid divorce.
  Includes bibliographical references.
  ISBN 978-1-59955-517-1
  1. Marriage. 2. Sexual division of labor. 3. Divorce. I. Title.
  HQ734.M713 2011
  646.7'8--dc22
                        2010051210

Cover design by Danie Romrell
Cover design © 2011 by Lyle Mortimer
Edited and typeset by Kelley Konzak

Printed in the United States of America

10 9 8 7 6 5 4 3 2 1

Printed on acid-free paper

# PRAISE FOR SHERRI MILLS and
*I Almost Divorced My Husband, but I Went On Strike Instead*

**Dr. Liz Hale, Licensed Marriage & Family Therapist:**

Sherri Mills is a true "head" expert! More clients have sat in her chair than in mine. Within the walls of her over 40-year, privately owned hair salon, heads are not only beautiful, they are wisely instructed.

Sherri Mills has become a household name, and rightly so as she sets out to change households for the better, one home at a time.

If you are frustrated and thinking of leaving your marriage, read Sherri's book! Don't change households, change *your* household! Start today.

**Dr. Angel Casey, Licensed Clinical Psychologist:**

Sherri has brought a new perspective to an insidious and destructive problem in our culture. I have worked with women who were chronically depressed, angry—even suicidal—over the double duty and double standard of householder work. . . .

I genuinely appreciate her sharing [her innovative solutions] with me. I've learned more from this little book than I have at some very expensive professional conferences.

**Dr. Karl Kraync, MS, CRC, NNC, LPC:**

Sherri's work is empowering, powerful, practical, and yet simple. When her book is published, I plan on assigning all of my marriage counseling clients to read the book after our first session.

**Mellie Patterson, Mental Health Professional LCSW:**

Sherri's book is an insightful and easy-to-read book about the plight many women experience in the role of homemaker. . . . As a mental health professional, I continue to hear similar stories from women who are struggling with depression and homemaker burnout. I am excited to be able to use the information contained in this book to help my clients as well as others . . . who are struggling.

**Sharon Madsen, teacher:**

As I sat in the client chair at the Risque Beauty Salon, Sherri not only made me beautiful on the outside, she counseled me through a very tumultuous situation, giving me eventual peace on the inside.

I encouraged Sherri to write this book, to help others as she has helped me—others who aren't lucky enough to live in the Risque Beauty Salon territory.

# CONTENTS

Foreword . . . . . . . . . . . . . . . . . . . . . . . . . . . . . . . . . . . . ix

Acknowledgments . . . . . . . . . . . . . . . . . . . . . . . . . . . . xi

Introduction. . . . . . . . . . . . . . . . . . . . . . . . . . . . . . . . . .1

1. Does This Sound Familiar? . . . . . . . . . . . . . . . . . . . . .3

2. The Rise of Householder Work . . . . . . . . . . . . . . . . .9

3. My Darkest Days . . . . . . . . . . . . . . . . . . . . . . . . . . . 11

4. Typical History of an Overworked Wife . . . . . . . . . . 15

5. Trying to Awaken Mr. Clueless . . . . . . . . . . . . . . . . 19

6. My Strike Preparations. . . . . . . . . . . . . . . . . . . . . . .25

7. I Went On Strike . . . . . . . . . . . . . . . . . . . . . . . . . . .29

8. Why "Help" Is a Four-Letter Word . . . . . . . . . . . . . .37

9. Both Men and Women Need Reeducating . . . . . . . . 45

10. The Real Cost of Divorce . . . . . . . . . . . . . . . . . . . . 51

11. The Rule of the Ruler . . . . . . . . . . . . . . . . . . . . . . . 61

12. Let's Analyze His Faults Too . . . . . . . . . . . . . . . . . 67

13. Communicate! . . . . . . . . . . . . . . . . . . . . . . . . . . . . 73

14. Strike Test . . . . . . . . . . . . . . . . . . . . . . . . . . . . . . . 81

15. Ministrike . . . . . . . . . . . . . . . . . . . . . . . . . . . . . . . 85

16. Full Strike . . . . . . . . . . . . . . . . . . . . . . . . . . . . . . . 87

17. Thoughts to Keep You Strong and Sustain Your Love. . . . . . . . 95

18. The Wrong Way to Strike. . . . . . . . . . . . . . . . . . . . 101

19. When Divorce Is Necessary . . . . . . . . . . . . . . . . . .107

# CONTENTS

20. Everything I Know about Chores
    I Learned from My Mother . . . . . . . . . . . . . . . . . . . . . . . . . 117
Epilogue. . . . . . . . . . . . . . . . . . . . . . . . . . . . . . . . . . . . . . . . . . 129
Appendix A: The Fair Marriage Contract. . . . . . . . . . . . . . . . . 131
Appendix B: Householder Chore Lists . . . . . . . . . . . . . . . . . . . 139
Appendix C: A Few Reminders . . . . . . . . . . . . . . . . . . . . . . . . . 157
Bibliography. . . . . . . . . . . . . . . . . . . . . . . . . . . . . . . . . . . . . . . . 161
About the Author. . . . . . . . . . . . . . . . . . . . . . . . . . . . . . . . . . . . 163

# FOREWORD

**IN OUR FAST-PACED SOCIETY,** marriage and family have become as disposable as fast food and diapers. It is easier to end a marriage where you find yourself unhappy than to work together to make lives and situations better and fair for all in the family. Disposable marriage has been the norm—until this book. Be ready to be reminded that if you loved someone once, you should be willing to fight to keep love alive.

I may be a Licensed Marriage & Family Therapist, topped off by a doctorate in clinical psychology; however, Sherri Mills, Psy-Cosmetologist, is the true "head" expert! More clients have sat in her chair than in mine.

Her therapy is free; mine isn't! Within the walls of her forty-five-year-old, privately owned hair salon, heads are not only beautified, they are wisely instructed.

Sherri Mills has become a household name to countless families in her community, and rightfully so as she sets out to change households for the better, one home at a time. Having worked with too many clients to mention, some extending from the same family and spanning three decades, Sherri has had a front-row seat on the before-and-after pictures of marriage, family, and even divorce. It's the harried and harrowing consequences of the latter that haunt her most—and that motivated her to write this book, based both on listening to the trials of her clients and on making some sweeping changes in her own marriage.

You see, when Sherri went on strike over two decades ago, she intuitively knew something that professionals would only begin to discover twenty years later: husbands who share in the load of housework are happier and healthier and live longer. Now, Sherri didn't necessarily go on strike for her husband's well-being; she did it to save her own sanity. Ill from the "wonder woman" syndrome, she had hit the wall in her marriage to a male chauvinist (albeit a loving one!).

Sherri brings a fresh perspective to that insidious and destructive problem in our culture—the unbearable pressure of being the lone ranger on the home front. With multiple roles, including chef, chauffeur, administrator, housekeeper, travel agent, zookeeper, counselor, consultant, comforter, organizer, provider, and professional shopper, she had grown physically weary, becoming an emotionally disheartened WIFE: Woman Ill From Everything!

This book should become a standard for all persons wishing to obtain a marriage license, for those who attend marriage classes, and for those in troubled marriages who are in counseling. The ideas in this book are empowering, powerful, practical, and yet simple.

If you are frustrated and thinking of leaving your marriage, read Sherri's book! Don't change households, change your household! Start today!

*Dr. Liz Hale, Licensed Marriage & Family Therapist*
*Clinical Psychologist*
*Salt Lake City, Utah*

# ACKNOWLEDGMENTS

**F**IRST AND FOREMOST, this book is dedicated with deepest love and appreciation to my wonderful husband, Gerald, who is comfortable enough in his own skin to let me tell this personal story. He was worth the effort and strain it took to go on strike. He has been behind my project 100 percent. This book could not have been written without his support.

I would like to thank my devoted daughter, Nicole, who spent an enormous amount of her time helping me with my original website when she really didn't have the time to spend and for insisting—to the point of nagging—that I write this book. She always had faith in my ability and knew this story had to be told. She even went as far as sending me the book *How to Get Published* and wrote, "Mom, one day millions of women will be indebted to you."

I owe Guy Dumas a debt of gratitude for gently convincing me that just because I didn't like the computer was no excuse for not writing this book. He told me I could do it all with pen and paper. I did just that.

My grandson Derek is to be congratulated for taking my chicken scratching and painstakingly transcribing it all onto the computer. He was there when I needed him, even if the work took him into the wee hours of the morning to finish.

I owe so much to my original editor, Bianca Dumas, for placing some of her own literary projects on hold to work with me. The professionalism she lent to my project cannot be put into words. She knew this story had to be told. My book never would have been finished without her professional help and prodding.

I am eternally grateful for the joy I have received from my best friends forever (they used to be my children), Guy and Chanda, Rod and Nancy, and Nicole and Mark.

I would like to express my appreciation to my sister Louise, who helped me tremendously with the "Teaching Children How to Work" section. Thank you, sis, for being the expert in that area.

I want to thank my grandchildren, Morgan, Derek, Bodie, Braidy, Hailey, Maegan, Hanna, Nathan, Kelsey, Mark, Carter, Dan, and Kyzer for being such wonderful rewards. They inspire me daily.

A special thanks to my other family—my clients. They gave me the material for this book by sharing their pain and vulnerability with me. They all knew they could trust me, and they can. The names and stories have been camouflaged. One person, however, chose to be uncovered. It can now be divulged that Marsha Bianco O'Shea was my coconspirator. She was my typist at the time of my secret strike.

The stars had to have been aligned when I found my current editor, Elaine Rhode. Finding her was a godsend. Her faith in my book and her expertise are immeasurable.

I would like to express my appreciation to Cedar Fort Publishing for accepting my book. Shersta Gatica, the acquisitions editor, was always there when I needed a question answered. Kelley Konzak, my new editor at Cedar Fort, gave me encouragement by telling me how wonderful it was that someone cared so much about the family. Emily Showgren has been so helpful in marketing my book. She has always been prompt in returning my emails. I feel like it was meant to be that it took so long to get a publisher; Cedar Fort seems to be the perfect fit.

To Dr. Liz Hale, who set me on the path to being published. She had enough faith in me to have me on her television show twice. She has my utmost respect and admiration. This woman is not only beautiful, a fantastic psychologist, and a TV personality, but she also shares my vision: trying to strengthen marriages for all children's sake. This wonderful woman is my hero.

# INTRODUCTION

**F**ROM THE PODIUM, I scanned the sea of faces in the crowd at a women's conference in Washington State. Partway through my speech, I focused on a woman with tears streaming down her face. She looked like so many I'd met and interviewed who were in the midst of marital burnout from doing it all—what psychologist Liz Hale calls "an insidious and destructive problem in our culture."

Why the tears? Was she sad because the whole situation seemed hopeless to her? Was she relieved because she could finally see that she wasn't alone? Were they happy tears because she could finally see a glimmer of hope for solving the age-old problem of household inequality?

After the speech, women lined up to thank me and to ask questions—young mothers, older women, and even grandmothers who said, "Where were you a long time ago when I really needed help?" or, "I wish I would have had this information before I got my divorce." The young woman who had been crying came up to talk to me too and said, "When is your book coming out? I really need it."

After I went on strike to save my marriage and my sanity, I discovered to my surprise that men really have no idea of the hardships we women go through when we work all day only to come home to another full-time job, one with no time off and no sick leave.

That was more than twenty years ago. Surely in this enlightened time, one would expect that relationships would be truly equal. But after interviewing women and children, numerous psychologists, and

1

some men in various western states, I sadly realized that the dynamic hasn't changed much at all.

If you doubt that, try this scenario: Picture a couple with full-time jobs and young children to parent. It takes hours to do the multitude of tasks to keep everything tidy and running smoothly in the household. What if none of it gets done this week, and suddenly you appear at the door, an unexpected guest. How likely is it that you would think, "Oh my! What an awful housekeeper that husband is."

Unfortunately, these "dark ages" extend to some professionals, those we turn to for advice. I interviewed a woman who was fed up with everything in her marriage. She was seriously thinking of taking her three children and leaving her husband. I convinced her to go to a counselor.

She did, and she told the counselor how her husband did absolutely nothing around the house.

The counselor responded by saying, "There must be an underlying problem, and if you think real hard, you will realize what it is." He also said, "Housework is just what is on the surface, and it is masking the real problem."

No! The fact that the husband is doing nothing around the house *is* the underlying problem, and it leads to fatigue, chronic depression, anger, hatred, and many women wanting out of a marriage that began with love.

I wrote this book because, in our society, most mothers who file for divorce over household inequality are young mothers with small children. These mothers have no idea that their marital problems are solvable without divorce. Instead, they find themselves and their children in worse straits than they ever imagined—after a divorce that didn't need to happen.

*Sherri Mills*

# 1

# DOES THIS SOUND FAMILIAR?

> A husband was disgusted because his wife was taking so long to get ready. She retorted, "Honey, I'll trade places with you next time. You get yourself and the kids ready and make sure we have everything we need and that the house is clean. I'll sit in the car and honk."

**H**ELEN LINGERED ON THE PORCH of her big, beautiful home. She had a headache again, and she didn't know what to do. "I can't take another second," she said to herself, thinking of the mess that grew in her house while her husband sat glued to a football game.

Helen spent the next few days visiting with a lawyer, and before the week was up, she had filed for divorce against Jim, the father of her four grade-school-aged children.

Jim was thrust into immobilizing shock. In his mind, he had a great marriage, had been a wonderful father, and worshipped his children. He made a living to support his family, loved his wife and kids, and had a lot of fun. He could think of nothing he could have done differently and wondered what kind of insanity could have gripped Helen.

Because of the enormous workload that was expected of her at home, Helen had been seething for years. She had been doing all the domestic work for so long—from laundry to paying bills to weeding the flower beds and getting the kids to all their appointments—that the love she had once felt for Jim was now a distant memory. In fact, Helen told me she never had loved Jim.

## HELEN'S REALITY

I was there in the beginning, so I knew how much she did love

3

Jim and how much they loved each other, yet I also knew the intense resentment she toted around with her daily. It was easy for me, seeing her overworked for years, to understand how she could forget her love. The fact was, Helen could deny that she had ever loved Jim, and this eased her guilt and also made it easier to explain to people why she was taking her children's father away from them.

Helen had told me everything. I have been a hairdresser for over forty years and had been hers for a decade. And as you know, people tell their hairdressers everything.

Under her denial, Helen felt guilt. She believed that everything that had gone wrong in her marriage was wholly her fault, and she did seem to have reason to believe that was so. Jim had always told her she spent way too much money at the grocery store because he had never gone shopping himself and to him, groceries cost what they did thirty years ago. When a shoe or a set of keys was lost around the house, Jim and the kids had always assumed that it was Helen's job to keep track of things and her fault if they couldn't be found. She was the only one who packed suitcases for trips, and if she forgot an item or packed the wrong one, well, of course she was to blame.

Nobody but Helen was ever to blame because nobody but Helen ever did any of the domestic work. She translated her frustration into hatred toward Jim and guilt for her children's unhappiness.

## WHAT ABOUT THE HUSBAND?

Helen and I had had countless discussions over the years about how unhappy she was and how she felt like a slave, so I wondered if Helen had ever told Jim how she felt. Or if she had, what had prevented him from hearing her and helping to make it better? Whatever had caused the gap made it easier for Helen to file for divorce than to approach Jim and try to fix things.

In the ensuing days, weeks, and months, I heard both sides of their story. They were both my clients. I had cut their hair for years, and it seemed both couldn't wait to talk to me.

## JIM'S REALITY

One Friday, Jim came in. I had made sure when he made his appointment that the salon would be empty so he could talk freely if he wanted to, and boy, did he want to. "She always said she was happy," he said. "She always told me she loved me and was always doing things for me." This statement sent a jolt to my inner sanctum. I knew how resentful she was for doing all those things, and he had taken it as a sign of her love.

"What things did you do for her?" I asked.

"Everything!" Jim snapped back, so quickly that I knew he must have had a few disappointments of his own. "I do everything for her. I work hard to support her and the kids. I bought her a coat for her birthday." He listed a few more half-yearly good deeds.

Jim looked at me in the mirror. "She never once told me she was unhappy," he said. "Until now, she never mentioned how my fishing and golfing bothered her. Or that she wanted me to help with the house and kids."

## HELEN'S PHILOSOPHY

I couldn't wait for Helen to come in because she had been complaining profusely to me for years.

"Jim said you have never told him any of the things you've told me," I said.

"I never have," Helen said matter-of-factly. "He should have known."

## AND THE CONSEQUENCES

I have seen this situation over and over again: one party is deliriously happy in a relationship and the other is seething. When one person doesn't voice her disappointment early on, the disappointment builds until it explodes into disaster. The lack of communication causes havoc in every aspect of the relationship.

The divorce went through, and although Helen got half the assets and child support, her life changed greatly. She had spent her younger years raising children and only working part-time jobs, so her career and skills were undeveloped. Her husband, while shaken and torn from the family he wanted, was in the middle of a thriving career and was financially set.

Helen, on the other hand, had to work full-time and overtime. Her responsibilities with the children magnified because now she was the sole parent in her household, and her children were struggling with their feelings after the divorce. She couldn't be there for them when they needed her because she was always working. Gone was the attendance at school functions, the hugs and greetings when the kids got home from school. Her children felt suddenly on their own and resented Helen for moving them from their big, beautiful home into "the dump," as they called their apartment.

Helen kept coming to me for haircuts, and the stories she told me got worse. She had felt relieved at the beginning of her divorce. "It's like a big load has been lifted off my shoulders," she'd said. She had enjoyed the attention she began to get on dates too. However, it didn't take Helen long to become discouraged about her new life.

"I got a phone call from Mark's teacher," she said one day while I was streaking her hair. "Mark has been sassing the teachers, using foul language, and beating up other kids at school." She started to cry. I could see why. Mark had been a gentle soul before the divorce. It had been unthinkable that he would even sass a teacher.

Helen's next visit to my salon came after she had remarried. Instead of hearing a honeymoon story, I got an earful about how her new husband had been verbally abusive to her children. "He seems to resent anything I do for them," she cried. "I just don't know what to do."

"He's a monster," she wailed at her next visit. "He actually blackened Brittany's eye."

"You called the police, didn't you?" I asked.

"Of course I did," Helen said. "He's been hitting the kids for a while, and I had him arrested. We're separated, and the kids live with their father for now. Which is great, because right now they hate me."

As the haircuts went on, I heard more and more. The kids moved back in with Helen because their father's new wife had demanded they leave. Her son David got into drugs and was in and out of jail, and Helen suspected Brittany of using drugs too. "She's completely out of hand," Helen said.

"What does Jim say about all of this?" I asked.

Helen looked at my reflection in the mirror. "He blames me," she said. "Because I chose to get divorced and then because of my choice for a second husband."

Helen is now with a third husband and seems moderately happy.

Just recently, though, Helen told me that if she had to do it all over again, she would have kept the family together and worked on her marriage. That didn't surprise me. Helen's wasn't the first divorce I had witnessed, and her outcome was so much like every other divorce I had seen.

## "RESEARCH ON LIFE" CHANGES MY LIFE

As a hairdresser, I have heard real-life problems and real-life outcomes, successes, and failures. I've had weekly and monthly sessions with my clients over periods of years or lifetimes. I have the advantage over professional counselors of sticking with clients through generations, so I see more than the result of the quick fix. I see them after their quick fixes have turned into nightmare rides, and all the while their children are hooked to the tailgate.

I spent the first part of my hairdressing career listening to clients' problems like Helen's and Jim's but keeping my big mouth shut. Sometimes I offered support, and I always kept their confidence.

After a few years of consistently cutting my clients' hair, I knew the pros and cons of every choice they'd make. I called it my "research on life." This increased my interest in relationships and personal growth, and I began a massive research campaign to read everything I could about these subjects, a passion I still exercise today. It became easier for me to know what to say to my clients when they asked for advice, because I knew what results they might have.

Often, when paying for a haircut, a client would joke, "Now, what do I owe you for my therapy session?"

I always felt fortunate to be able to see the consequences of my clients' divorces, and the lessons I learned became one of the reasons I decided not to file for divorce during the low points of my marriage. Over and over again, I saw too many dream solutions turn into nightmares. I knew that divorce would not be an option for me. I'll tell you why:

1.  Most women haven't yet learned how to fix the problem of overwork, so the chances of the same situation coming up in a subsequent marriage are enormous.
2.  You continue doing it all but now have to navigate your children's relationships with a new father figure. Sometimes those relationships work out. Very often they don't.
3.  If you have a good man who simply adores his children, it seems like a no-brainer to keep him and work your heart out to fix whatever is wrong.

Now, I want you (and the world) to know that before you pull the plug on your marriage, there are many alternatives. I have never seen a mother with young children find a better life after divorce except in the case of abuse in a marriage. Most divorced young mothers experience the same disappointments they had before divorce except that shortly after a second marriage, they also have to deal with stepparenting and jealousy from the new spouse. My heart breaks for the children who have to live between parents whose relationship has fallen apart. These children are my clients too, and I hear about their suffering firsthand.

My hope is to somehow reach those women whose relationships haven't fallen apart yet. There are ways to heal a relationship, provided it is free from physical or emotional abuse. The love can be brought back when unacknowledged problems are brought to the surface and worked on in the right way.

# 2

# THE RISE OF
# HOUSEHOLDER WORK
## AND WHY IT NEEDS A SOLUTION

> The family's week was typically hectic, and the house remained uncleaned. You are the unexpected guest. Would you think, "Oh, my! This husband is a terrible housekeeper"?

**T**HROUGH MY YEARS OF listening to clients' lives, I learned that one of the biggest problems in marriages is the problem Helen and Jim had: the imbalance of householder work. I call it "householder work" because everyone in the household should carry an equal amount of the burden.

Women and men both assume that householder work belongs to women from the outset. Even educated and modern women believe this. The idea is deeply embedded in our culture and psyches. Women and men don't talk about the division of labor, and that means they haven't made plans for dividing it. When the consequences of the imbalance are felt, most people have no idea how to have a conversation about this crazy-making topic that angers them so deeply. As a result, the husband and wife both make assumptions.

## THE STRATEGY FOR YOU IN THIS BOOK

In this book, you will discover that assumptions don't work. Neither does blaming or self-pity. Quite to the contrary, these tactics doom all relationships. There are good ways to communicate. There are things

9

you can say and do to get what you want from your marriage, and I will tell you what those things are.

You will discover how we got to the place where women are over-worked at home, so much so that they resent their husbands. It's the status quo, but you'll see that you can change it. You can rediscover lost love or maintain the love you have, even as you work out a change.

The first third of this book gives you my personal story and the stories of others who have been through divorce. Rather than leave my husband and children, I went on strike against them. I prepared myself and my contract until everything was in place, waiting for the right time. My strike lasted more than a week, and everyone thought I was crazy, but it was a phenomenal and lasting success. After the strike, the workload in our household became balanced. I no longer felt like the family slave. I had more time to spend connecting with my husband and appreciating him, and the love between us began to grow once again.

Through my experience, you will learn all the options you have for improving your marriage. You may not have to go on a full-blown strike, but I'll show you how to do that too, if it's obvious that your problems need a big fix.

I want women to know that the realities of divorce make it a poor option.

I was a young mother once, so I know some women won't have time to read this book front to back. I've designed it so you can read it in the bathroom, in the doctor's waiting room, and while you're standing at the sink eating your peanut butter sandwich.

The second third of the book is organized by topics to help you analyze your marriage and learn how you can strengthen it, with tips and reminder summaries at the end of each chapter.

The last third and the appendixes concentrate on whether or not striking is best for you or if a ministrike will do, and thoughts to keep you strong and loving if you decide to strike. At the end of the book, you'll find the Fair Marriage Contract and lists of chores. These will give you a starting point for asking your husband to take on more of the householder work so you can have a fair and joyful marriage.

# 3

# MY DARKEST DAYS

"He should have known!"

**I** REMEMBER SO WELL the day my husband, Gerald, came home from work to find me sick. Again. He had the same disappointed look on his face that I had seen so many times before. "How do you feel?" he asked. The question came across like a phrase on a broken record that had been playing for years.

Like that same broken record, I flatly replied, "Fine."

Gerald, however, could tell that I wasn't fine, and being the man who feels helpless if he can't fix everything, he decided to offer his unwanted advice. Again.

"Do you think if you changed your diet or something like that you could get better?" he asked, concerned but also annoyed. He had come home again to a house that was less than clean, a late dinner that was less than wonderful, and three children who were tugging at his trousers for his attention because they hadn't been getting much from me that day.

"You're always sick," he said with a little less concern and a lot more frustration than he would have liked to portray.

That statement stuck in my craw. I had heard it one too many times, and I just exploded.

"You bet I'm sick all the time!" I shouted. "And do you know why I'm sick all the time?"

He nodded his head in the affirmative as if he were preparing himself for what was coming.

"It's because I'm not a man!" I screeched. "I don't have time to get well like you do. This sickness I have is called being a woman." I gritted my teeth, warming up. I wanted Gerald to know that it wasn't just me, that there were a lot of women like me whose bodies had been destroyed by childbirth and who had never really recovered. I wanted him to hear this because it felt so isolating to think that I was the only one, and I knew it couldn't be true. Unfortunately, I was so out of control with my sadness and fury that I just opened my mouth and raged, whether I made sense or not.

"Unlike you men," I yelled, crying, "we women start getting sick at age twelve. That's when we start our periods and get severe PMS every month." This subject was sure to turn Gerald's ears off, but I wasn't thinking of that.

"But," I said, gritting my teeth, "that's just preparing us for pregnancy and nine months of projectile vomiting. Then when the baby finally comes, we have trouble with the delivery and have to have a blood transfusion. But guess what?" I sneered. "We women don't go home from the hospital and rest. We have a baby who is up all night, and we just have to keep marching on, no matter how we feel."

Gerald started moving away, thinking I was finished with my tirade, but I had only just begun.

"Then another pregnancy with nine months of puking my guts out." I got louder and louder and more out of control with each sentence. "Then two babies in diapers, and guess what happens next?"

By now Gerald was prepared for however long this outburst was going to take, but he had a glazed look on his face. How could he respond to me, anyway? I was angry, I was crazy, and I was determined to get my point across, whether I was actually communicating well or not. My shrill message continued, but I spoke the words into a void.

"What happens next is two babies in diapers and nine more months of bile being ripped from the pit of my stomach!"

I was screaming and crying at the same time, and from the look on Gerald's face, I was certain he was now very concerned: he not only had a sick wife, but she was mentally deranged as well.

"So tell me, Mr. Macho," I continued, "what kind of sickness came through your body to make this family?"

I didn't wait for an answer. I just turned on my heels, stomped into the bedroom, slammed the door, and immersed myself deep into a gloomy cloud of self-pity.

I couldn't believe how unfair life was that one gender had to suffer for it all. I was so angry at Gerald, as if it were all his fault.

Even then it didn't occur to me to ask for help. I was just so angry at him because he didn't automatically know what I was feeling and how to help me.

# 4

# TYPICAL HISTORY
# OF AN OVERWORKED WIFE

"If we watch football together, where will the clean laundry come from?"

**WHAT WAS IT THAT** made me take over every household duty in the beginning? Even then, in 1967, there were women who were demanding equality from their husbands. But I knew a few of them, and from what I saw, those wives (in my town, anyway), were acting like selfish people. They seemed too demanding at home, and they berated their husbands in public. That constant nitpicking wasn't a bit attractive to me. What was more, I was proud of my big, strong husband, a man's man who would never put up with that, and I knew that the kind of man I married would never have patience with a demanding attitude from me, nor would he ever sit back and allow me to put him down in public.

I think what caused me to overwork in those days is what causes women to overwork today.

I had just gotten married. I had all the energy in the world. I also had a competitive nature and was out to prove that I could be just as good a wife, or a better one, than my friends, my mother, or my mother-in-law.

I had the desire to have it all—I wanted to work, have more money, and have my kids and a perfect house too. And because I never saw my dad work on the domestic front, I believed my husband shouldn't have to. My husband and many others held that same belief.

In my case, Gerald didn't want me to work outside our home either. He wanted to take care of me because that's how he believed it should be done. I, however, was a career person and would have none of it. I loved being creative with hair and interacting with clients, and I was emphatic about continuing it. The importance of my career became a very touchy subject and the very thing most of our arguments were about. And that became the launchpad to my first big mistake.

I finally convinced Gerald that I could keep everything going on the home front even as I worked. I had to prove I could do it.

And I did. I would cook a hot breakfast and fix Gerald's lunch in the mornings. I always had dinner on the table when Gerald got home. I did all of the housework by myself and all of the yard work after Gerald got a second job. That's when all of the work—inside and outside the house—became my job permanently. There were times Gerald would do little things around the house, but I would secretly do them over because I thought he hadn't done them well enough.

## TRAPPED BY MY OWN "SUCCESS"

After the children came along, I wanted Gerald's help, and I was happy for him to get things done, no matter how poorly. By then, however, I had really blown it. I had set myself up as the woman who did everything and as the woman everyone needed every minute of the day.

Like an idiot, I had established the routine of getting Gerald's breakfast on the table before I went to work at five or five-thirty in the morning. When the children came along, still trying to be the super woman, I continued to get up early and fix a hot breakfast for all. The kids would just move their food around their plates more than they'd eat it, and I'd end up feeding the food to the dog.

It wasn't until the two older children were in school that I came to the conclusion that a healthy breakfast didn't do the kids any good in the dog's belly. I finally allowed them to have cold cereal. The only one unhappy about this transition was the dog.

Ironically (but I'm sure you'll understand), having three kids under six, a full-time job, and a husband who didn't help meant that I didn't have time to teach the kids to help. It was easier and faster to do everything myself.

When it came to deep cleaning, Gerald thought it was unnecessary. So, when he went fishing or hunting—even when he went on his annual two-week hunting trip every fall—I would be happy about it and secretly look forward to getting my walls washed, cupboards cleaned, and carpets shampooed while he was gone.

Just writing this down makes me realize what a road map to exhaustion I had created for myself.

I think that for wives of that era, it was a somewhat universal experience. Women were overworked, but they were beginning to want a way out.

## DIVORCE—THE SOLUTION?

In the minds of my clients in the beauty shop, divorce was a solution they used liberally. They would tell me how resentful they had become of "doing it all," to the point that they desperately wanted out of their marriages. When I would suggest a few little things to do to make their situations better, they would sadly look at me as if this was their lot in life. I didn't understand. Why would women who were so desperate, unhappy, and disillusioned think divorce was the only solution? Especially when they had children?

But I'm getting ahead of myself. Although I had suffered household overwork for thirteen years, I did not want a divorce. The problem of being overworked and underappreciated was a challenge, but what saved my marriage was my belief that divorce would never be a solution.

# 5

# TRYING TO AWAKEN
# MR. CLUELESS

"How often do we go to bed at night feeling the comfort and love of our wives and lovers, but knowing them so little that we do not recognize the burden they bear?"

—Sey Chassler, *Parade Magazine*

**I TRIED EVERYTHING** I could think of to change my situation and make my home life more fair, including a little plan of letting the work pile up for a week to see if Gerald would notice and wonder why there was a mess.

In my plan, I went to work, he went to work, and the kids continued their normal disorderly conduct. The only chore I did was to fix meals and do enough dishes for the next meal. After a few days of disarray and the weekend approaching, I wanted to force Gerald to notice the mess. Saturday afternoon and Sunday were the only days I had to put everything back together before another week of work started.

So Friday evening after everyone was in bed I got up, tiptoed into the other room, emptied both hampers and loosely spread the dirty clothes all over the floor, down the steps, and all the way into the laundry room. I put the last of the dirty clothes right in front of the furnace in a huge ugly pile.

Very early the next morning I awoke and leaned over to Gerald. "Ger," I whispered. "I heard a noise coming from the furnace. Could you go see if there's anything wrong?"

To his credit, he was always the fixer for major malfunctions. He sleepily walked down the stairs to check the furnace.

I was already congratulating myself. *What an ingenious plan*, I thought. *This weekend I'm going to get a lot accomplished in the house because I'll have help from Gerald and the children.*

I lay there flat on my back, blanket pulled up tight in anticipation. I thought that when Gerald got back upstairs and complained about the mess I'd have a hundred responses ready. "Well, I work too, and I can't clean everything up by myself," I'd say. Or, "If you don't like how it looks, then you pick it up." Or, "Have the kids help you clean up and surprise me when I get home." I thought I'd finally found a way to change my life.

After a few clings and clanks I could hear Gerald ascending the stairs.

I waited with bated breath.

"There's nothing wrong with the furnace," he said as he nestled back inside the covers and buried his head in the pillow. In seconds he was fast asleep.

I abruptly sat up in bed and felt like the girl in the exorcist movie whose head would not stop spinning.

I went to work and made another plan. I would call Gerald on the phone, bring up the furnace problem, and then discuss the mess directly.

I asked, "What did you think of the rubble you had to navigate around?"

His answer made the tension in my body turn to pure mush.

He said, "What rubble?"

When this plan didn't work, I still tried to get help—I ranted and raged, cried and felt sorry for myself. I complained that the children made nothing but messes and that they didn't know how to help out or contribute. This just led Gerald to think I didn't enjoy being a mother. At one point, he actually thought that I wished I had never had the children, which was not the case. I just had too many responsibilities, no downtime, and no way to communicate that fact.

## POEM FALLS ON DEAF EARS

Finally I tried writing a poem to get his attention. I wanted to show him something funny enough to grab his interest but real enough to make him get it. I filled the poem with calamities—real, everyday calamities that happen when you have small children.

> The perils of being a mother
> Are not equal to any other.
> For granted she's taken
> And often mistaken
> For a robot. "She'll do it. Why bother?"

This was the beginning of a lengthy poem I wrote so Gerald would get the message. I called it, "The Mother's Lament." Here are another few stanzas:

> As mom is changing the baby,
> The other kids are thinking, "Maybe
> She'll be busy awhile."
> To each other they smile
> Then she hears one kid holler, "Don't spray me!"

> She takes that brief moment to swear
> And proceeds to pull out her hair.
> Then she feels like a dope,
> And she snarls, "I can cope,"
> But she secretly thinks it's not fair.

> Her duties are started again,
> With the hope that she has at least ten
> Minutes to get things done.
> But there's not even one:
> It's lunchtime now, Old Mother Hen.

> The lunch turns up half on the floor,
> And they turned up their noses once more.
> As usual, she fixed it,
> And as usual, they nixed it,
> And then in an hour they want more.

The poem is riddled with more and more disasters, most of which actually happened the day I wrote the poem. No mother would believe that, would they?

The last part of the poem examines where the husband is coming from when he comes home and finds chaos. He immediately realizes that there's a problem, but he can't believe this is the kind of thing that goes on regularly with normal little children and a normal exhausted wife on the premises.

No, the husband assumes that the problems arise because of something his wife is doing wrong. His reaction is to blame her, at first for being too crabby and then later for being too lax. Finally, he just takes five himself:

After supper she wails to her spouse,
"I've got to get out of this house!
I think you will find
I'm losing my mind,
And, yes, this is blood on my blouse!"

Then Hubby starts pulling his rank
And says, "Dear, I'll be truly frank.
When the children don't mind
I am sure you will find
It's because you are being a crank.

"Now, as for you losing your mind
That's silly. Sit down and unwind.
It's not really so bad,
I think you should be glad
You don't have to put up with my grind.

"If you did, would you ever get tough.
So you think that you've got it rough
Staying home all the day
With the kids. By the way,
Could you please keep them out of my stuff?

"Hey, keep that kid quiet in there!
And get this one out of my hair!
They need a good whacking,
Your discipline is lacking!
I think I'll go get me some air."

I thought Gerald would recognize himself immediately when he read my poem. I thought he'd feel sorry for me, recognize the mistakes he was making, and immediately offer to help. Instead, he must have just pretended to read it. Years later, I found out he didn't even remember the poem.

## THE ORIGIN OF THE CONTRACT

I tried so many schemes, but none of them even made an impression on this relaxed, carefree man whom—without being aware of it—I had inadvertently helped to create.

I finally came to the conclusion that the only way to reach him was to deal with him on a level he would understand.

Gerald worked in the office of a clothing factory, where most of the other employees were members of a union. So he dealt with union contracts on a regular basis. I decided that I needed a contract that would protect me from company abuse. If you think about it, a housewife has the same type of job as a union employee—she does physical labor. She also does it without any of the benefits or pay and with a lot more responsibility and higher expectations. This is also a job where an employer (call him "husband") hires an employee (call her "wife"), whose job initially appears to be a fairly easy one. Then as the wife comes to the startling realization that this position was not only monstrously more than she bargained for, she also realizes that it provides very few benefits like free time, coffee breaks, or vacation hours. The normal thing to do in this situation would be to abruptly quit and get a job that can be done in eight hours and pays well.

But there's a problem.

She's signed a contract (the marriage contract), and there are other obstacles (love and children). So the wife does the next best thing to quitting. She goes to her boss and explains that the position she's in was not explained to her beforehand. Furthermore, she says, in order to do it properly, she needs help.

## WALK A MILE IN HER SHOES

But because the husband hasn't been in her shoes yet, he has absolutely no concept of the extent of her responsibilities. They had never been explained to him either. He is, in fact, still carrying around preconceived notions of what this easy job of housewifery is supposed to be, and he thinks she's crazy and totally inept.

She tries other ways of convincing him that she needs help, but to no avail.

Then she has a baby, then another baby, and another. Morning sickness with all three takes a tremendous toll. Suddenly, she is so busy that she doesn't even have time to wonder what to do about her problem anymore. Things simply get worse, and her child rearing years become years where she's in limbo. She can't go anywhere or do anything without first getting the children ready, and that tends to be more trouble than the outing is worth. Or she can hire a babysitter, but that's usually more than their budget will allow, and it becomes much easier to stay home. The result is that the wife becomes a hermit.

But the husband is not about to become a hermit. He perceives that his wife has become boring, stale, sickly, and lazy, since all she has to do all day is stay home with the kids. This is when criticism arrives in the relationship because if the wife is doing it all, then everything that goes wrong is also her fault.

# 6

# MY STRIKE PREPARATIONS

*Is this all there is?* I wondered. *Is this what I'm going to be doing for the rest of my life?* No way!

**I REALIZED THAT WE HAD** a problem in our marriage from the very beginning, but I put my problem away and worked at raising my kids. Then when my children started school, I finally had time to think. I thought and thought and thought. And woe to the husband who isn't used to a wife who thinks and then wakes up one day to find a wife who has thought too much.

"Is this all there is?" I wondered. "Is this what I'm going to be doing for the rest of my life?"

No way!

The only thing I could do was come up with a foolproof plan to change things because it would be either that or a divorce. So I came up with a plan: I went on strike. It was the hardest thing I have ever done, but the payoff is continuing every day: I have my original husband, who is now an angel. My children got to live with their own father, and my grandchildren have the best grandpa anyone could ever ask for.

Some of my best friends and clients were in the same boat and are now divorced and forced to deal with stepfamilies. Ironically, those women are still doing it all.

## A PLAN IN LANGUAGE A MAN UNDERSTANDS

Using a union contract as a guide, I began writing my marriage and householder contract (now called a Fair Marriage Contract, appendix A). I knew one thing for certain. Gerald understood union contracts.

He knew that workers used a contract as a negotiating tool and that if they didn't get at least some of the compensations they wanted in the negotiations, the workers would go on strike. That was my plan.

I had been negotiating for thirteen years to no avail, so a strike was inevitable—Gerald would actually understand that once I put it in front of him. I had to be ready to go on strike, professionally and calmly, in the way that Gerald was used to workers doing in the company. Before I went on strike, though, I had to have my contract completely prepared.

## THOROUGH PLANNING IS CRITICAL

Think about it. How successful do you think a union strike would be if the union members went through with a walkout before all the planning and demands were finished and ready to go? I took all of this into consideration before continuing my endeavor.

I could not take a chance on Gerald discovering my intentions before the contract was complete and professional. I also knew it would fail if it was presented at the wrong time, before I was mentally able to follow through. In fact, I had created a personal checklist to keep myself on track:

1. The contract had to be completely self-explanatory to eliminate any extra, unnecessary conversation. This would leave no room for arguments or loss of composure. It would eliminate any possibility of my being put on the defensive.
2. It had to be a strong proposal leaning to my side. This would make room for negotiations.
3. It had to be universal and cover every conceivable problem. This would be the only time to have the complete and undivided attention of the entire family, so nothing could go unstated.
4. It had to answer all the questions. How will we divide the householders' work? When? For exactly how long would the contract go on? What can we expect? Will negotiations be allowed, and how?
5. The contract itself had to portray strength and fortitude on my part, leaving no room for slip-ups or put-downs.

The difficult part was that the whole thing had to be completely finished and ready to use before Gerald had any idea of its existence, which meant I had to keep my notes and ideas hidden. I put each piece of paper, napkin, or envelope I had written on in separate places all around the house and tried to remember later where I put each note. I could not take a chance that he would find out about my contract and strike before I was ready. Finished and "professionally written," the contract would be intense and serious, and it would hold a lot of weight.

If Gerald had found any of it while I was in the process of jotting down my ideas, it might have given him a reason for ridicule and would certainly spoil my plan when I was ready to go on strike. The whole idea was to convince him that I was in his world, and ideas written on envelopes or toilet tissue would have vaulted me right back into my world, a world he perceived as simplistic, girlish, and jumbled.

I was getting myself into something enormous. I knew it and was willing to add more work to my already too busy life if it meant there would be a light at the end of the tunnel. What I wanted most was my fairy tale: a lifetime of happiness with the man of my dreams.

Back then I had no typewriter or computer and had to borrow one. I typed the contract in bits and pieces. As soon as I was finished with a page, I would hide it, as I'd done with my little notes. Wow, did I ever breathe a sigh of relief when the Fair Marriage Contract was completed.

## HAVE A BACKUP PLAN

I also had to have a backup plan ready in case Gerald wouldn't sign the contract and the strike got unbearable. Then I made another backup plan in case the first one didn't work.

I decided that if the strike got ugly, I would go stay at my mother's house (in another town) until Gerald and I could reach a decision. If that didn't make him think about signing the contract, I'd get some picket signs and march up and down the street, letting everyone know that I was a wife and mother on strike. But I'd do both of these things calmly, if I had to do them at all. I had to have a sense of equilibrium about me so I wouldn't get angry or lose my composure even if my strike created any kind of mess or any feeling of uncertainty or resentment from my husband, kids, or neighbors.

After the contract was finished, I put it away in a file at the beauty salon to save until I knew I was absolutely ready to go through with the strike.

# 7

# I WENT ON STRIKE

## EIGHT DAYS OF STAYING STRONG

> The payoff continues: I have my original husband, who is now an angel. My children got to live with their own father, and my grandchildren have the best grandpa anyone could ever ask for.

THE DAY CAME. I will remember it forever. I had sent the children to the store to get some things I needed for dinner while I was busy with daily chores, the busyness magnified because it was my only day off. The store was only a couple of blocks away, so it shouldn't have taken the boys any time at all to get there and back. Well, about forty-five minutes later, they came sauntering in, discarding the grocery sack on the table and going on their way. As I peered into the paper sack, I immediately noticed the wrong contents. I stopped both of them in their tracks. I demanded to know why they bought the wrong items and why something so easy had taken so long.

As usual, Gerald immediately jumped to their defense. "If it's so important for you to get the exact thing," he said, "you ought to get it yourself instead of having the kids do your job."

I could feel the anger seething through my body. This was the moment that made up my mind. *This is the time*, I thought. I now had the reassurance that no matter what happened, my strike would go into effect, and I would never give up.

It was obvious: I was married to a handsome, well-rounded man who made me laugh daily. He was a playful father who adored his children and was the life of the party when we were out with our friends. He never missed work, was very dedicated to his family, and was a super . . . male chauvinist.

## MY STRIKE ULTIMATUM

I abruptly ceased anything I was doing, including finishing the cooking I had started. I left the mess that the half-finished supper had splattered all over the kitchen and stated firmly, "Not only am I not going to the store, but as of this very second I am officially on strike and don't intend to do anything."

Gerald started to laugh. "Oh," he said with a half-sneer, half-chuckle. "And how do you propose to do that?"

"I have it all written out," I said, very calm but resolute. "And we don't need to discuss it any further because every possible answer to any questions you have will be found in the file at the beauty salon along with the contract."

I think it was curiosity more than anything that made Gerald get in the car and go down to the salon.

He was gone for what seemed like an eternity.

While he was gone, I was visualizing how bad the house would look for the entire duration of the strike. I had secretly decided to keep everything picked up on the landing by the front door so visitors would not immediately be aware of the disarray. I also planned to lock myself in the bathroom so I could keep the toilet clean. I knew my husband and children wouldn't notice I had scrubbed the toilet because everybody thought the tooth fairy did that job, anyway.

There was a perfect silence in the house. My children's eyes were asking all sorts of questions, but not a word was spoken.

When Gerald finally came home, there was more silence. I was glued to the couch, pretending to watch TV, and all I could hear in the kitchen were the clanging of pans and the clattering of someone setting the table. I was dumbstruck by what had just taken place, and I was a nervous wreck waiting to see what would happen next.

"Daddy said to come and eat," my daughter said.

## STAY FOCUSED—DON'T GIVE IN TO GESTURES

I slowly walked out to the kitchen and was greeted by a beautifully set table, napkins in place, and my three children sitting in their places, not daring to speak. Pork chops, mashed potatoes, and a beautiful salad adorned the table. There was even pudding for dessert, and the mess from cooking was all cleaned up. Millions of thoughts were rushing through my head, and the first thing I actually wanted to do was give

Gerald a hug, tell him I loved him, and say everything was okay.

I knew I couldn't. I had been here before. Gerald never meant to say or do anything to make things hard for me. I knew that. Besides, he had the personality that could charm the feathers right off a chicken. Inside I was trying to melt, but my head took charge, and I walked back to the TV after supper. It felt like walking a mile with cement in my shoes.

I don't know what was going on in Gerald's mind, but the silence was still deafening. I was thinking that he was probably seething inside. But I knew if I gave in now, everything would go back to the way it was in a few short days. I kept telling myself, "You've got to keep going. All your work cannot be for nothing." The most inspirational thing I repeated to myself was, "He will be worth the effort."

Filled with anticipation, I didn't sleep that night: what would the next day bring?

To my surprise, the same thing happened. Gerald fixed breakfast and enlisted the kids to help clean up. They all went through the house, vacuuming and making beds. When Gerald came from work, he started supper again. I was in perpetual shock. I had prepared for a mess, but not for this. The hardest thing I had to do was to get up from the table after eating a fantastic meal (far better than I'd have cooked) and make that long trip back to the couch. I spent the whole time there, not lifting a finger for any reason except to go to the salon. I didn't answer any of the children's questions and told them to call their dad if they had a problem.

## STORM BREWING—STAY CALM

On the third day of the strike, I knew something was afoot because first my son Guy sidled past the door, peered in, and then went on his way hurriedly, like he was getting out of the way. Then my daughter, Nicole, stood by the door as if to warn me of something, and I could hear loud stomping footsteps coming up the stairs.

"If you think for one minute that you are going to tell me what to do, you're crazy," Gerald bellowed. He was angrier than I had seen him in a long time. I don't remember the rest of the tirade because I was busy talking to myself in my head. *Hang in there*, I told myself, *He's worth it.* I kept reminding myself not to get angry back at him. *I can't get mad. I must stay strong. It's almost over. You've come this far. He's worth all the trouble.* The sounds in my head were even louder than Gerald's voice.

I must have internalized my intention not to get angry because I very calmly stated that I had worked on my strike way too long to allow it to fail. I let him know that no matter what, I would never quit. I told him about my backup plans and saw the shock on his face, especially when I mentioned marching up and down the street as he had seen union members do a few times. In truth, I would have been equally horrified if I had needed to carry out my marching plan. Such a protest wasn't like me, but he knew I meant it.

My bottom line remained solid: staying with this man for a lifetime was certainly worth the effort. I repeated to him that this was my ultimate reason for the strike and the contract.

I reminded him of his friends whose wives had asked their husbands for help. These men had refused and had found themselves in divorce court. I let him know that I had the man I wanted and was willing to do whatever it took to keep him.

## HANG IN THERE FOR SINCERITY!

After that, Gerald actually wanted to sign the contract, but he would certainly have been doing it insincerely.

I insisted the contract was not going to be signed until I was certain that Gerald had read the whole thing and understood it completely. I could tell by his attitude that he just wanted to get me off his back. He wasn't at all sincere. He hadn't even read the whole contract, and all my work would have been for nothing if I had let him sign it—he wouldn't have committed to the division of labor I'd proposed. The contract wasn't a legal document, so I couldn't actually force him to do anything he signed up for, and we would have had to struggle all over again.

The only way it could work was that after he read the whole contract and empathetically understood it, he would have to meet with the kids and explain to them what their part was. I had allowed them to skip out on all householder work just as I had their father, and that had to be remedied too. Only then would we negotiate.

## CHILDREN'S REACTION

Although the children were stunned and curious most of the time, all three had their combative moments.

Nicole came up to me one day and quite nastily stated, "I can't believe what you're making Dad do. How would you like to do it all plus go to work?" *Well, duh*, I thought.

Then Rod took his turn. "Lanny Turner said you're stupid for going on strike."

I patted his head and asked very firmly, "Do you really want to know what I think about what Lanny Turner is saying?"

Guy was the oldest and was extremely embarrassed, and he just leered at me a lot.

## BREAKTHROUGH

After a little over a week of coming home from work and then taking care of everything at home, Gerald came to me and said, "Tell the kids to be here when I get home." Very compassionately, he continued, "We need to change some things. Have the contract ready."

"Are you sure?" I asked. I felt in that moment that I loved him more than was possible. "I bet you're exhausted."

"I am," Gerald said. "But the sad thing about all of this is, you have done it all along."

When the kids were home, Gerald sat them down at the table, and I brought out the contract. We divided fifty-two chores among two adults and three children. Gerald would be totally responsible for the basement, outdoor chores, lawn, garbage, and garage. If he got home from work first, he would fix dinner. The children took on the responsibility for doing their own laundry and cleaning their rooms, and they also took on one extra chore. We even divided the vacation chores right then and there. Everyone signed the contract, and we ended with tears and a big hug.

## HE UNDERSTOOD

The first thing I remember happening after the strike was Rod running up the stairs and demanding, "Mom, where is my blue shirt? I need it today!"

Gerald wasted no time getting to the top of the steps, putting his finger in Rod's face, and answering, "Do you realize your mom has her own clothes to keep track of? She hasn't got time to keep track of four more peoples' clothes. Now, you go and find your own shirt."

I just about fell over with happiness.

Vacations changed too. Our family has always loved to go camping, but I used to be the one who packed, did all the cooking and cleaning during the camping trip, and unpacked and cleaned again when we arrived home. But the first camping trip after the strike was different. Gerald instructed the kids to pack their own clothes before we left. He and the kids helped me pack the trailer and prepare the food. Then, at that beautiful, green, mountain campsite, Gerald took on the role of chief cook. On the drive home, he reminded everyone what they were supposed to bring in from the truck or trailer so that we all had an equal amount of work to do.

## AN AWAKENING FOR BOTH OF US

It was through my own transition from an overworked and angry wife to a fairly worked and happy wife that I came to the startling conclusion that men don't put their wives in this terrible position on purpose. Nor did Gerald cave in and become whipped by a striking wife.

My strong, masculine man started out the strike trying to prove he could do everything better than I had, and ultimately realized what a monstrous endeavor it was. When he realized what I put up with day after day, he was horrified and even wanted to change the situation for me. In fact, he never even knew I was suffering until I let him experience my workload for himself.

## PUBLIC AFTERMATH

A few months after my life-changing strike, I received a call from Nancy Hobbs from the *Salt Lake Tribune*, wondering if she could do a story on our family. I told her I would have to ask my husband and figured that would be the end of it.

Gerald had always been comfortable in his own skin. He was also carrying around a newfound respect he had for me. He said, "Go for it."

Before we knew it, there was a full-page story on the front page of the Sunday home section of the *Salt Lake Tribune*. On the morning that paper came out, my phone rang off the hook. Friends, clients, and some strangers called to express respect for what Gerald had done.

One of my good friends came into the salon and said, "Sherri, I just want you to know that Gerald is one heck of a guy." Then she added, "My husband's even doing better because he's afraid I'll go on strike too. I wish you could keep it public longer so he would keep chipping in."

The positive reaction was way over 95 percent. The backlash came from a few friends and a couple of his relatives.

Lanny Turner sarcastically said to Gerald, "Why don't you tell your wife to teach the coal miners how to go on strike?"

Then another of his friends said, "How could you let her do that to you?"

A cousin called and said, "Gerald, I guess you know you have betrayed us all."

I had so many women thanking me and stating their tremendous respect for Gerald that the backlash hardly mattered to me. I just considered the source.

At first Gerald was sure to tell his entire group of detractors that women do a heck of a lot more work than men think they do and they deserve to be treated as equals. As time went on, however, he got real tired of folks stopping him at the store or on the street. Whether it was because they were proud of him or mad at him, it still began to wear him down until the embarrassing attention eventually faded. But despite all the publicity and his reactions to it, not once did he say that he wished I hadn't gone on strike.

## STILL HAPPY AND BALANCED YEARS LATER

I went on strike over twenty-five years ago, but the strike has been successful to this day. Gerald and I are happy and balanced. We do things for each other and with each other, and we love each other. Nancy Hobbs, who interviewed us in the *Tribune*, said we seemed like newlyweds. Yes, it was true; we felt like newlyweds.

Although I solved my problem over twenty-five years ago, women are having the same problem today—they tell me so. Young mothers with children and older retired women alike complain to me when they sit in my beauty shop chair, regretting that they have to do it all and their men just don't get it.

Now, I have an answer for them. "Listen," I tell them before I put them under the hair dryers. "You don't have to divorce your husband. You can be happy together again. Let me tell you how."

# 8

# WHY "HELP" IS A
# FOUR-LETTER WORD

> "Help" is a favor you do for someone when it's convenient for you or if you feel like doing it. Someone else is still responsible for the work.

**S**HARON WAS A YOUNG mother with three rambunctious children. She had been complaining to me for years how impossible it was to work all day and then come home and do everything in the house, much less do it well. She only complained to her husband, Nathan, in bits and pieces, and she told me she was afraid she'd start a fight if she really let him know how she felt. Nathan was also my client, and I asked Sharon a number of times if she wanted me to approach the subject with him. She said "no" for quite a while—even as she continued to complain to me. One day she finally said to me, "Go ahead, if you think it will help."

By this time, my salon services had evolved into a kind of hairdressing/social work combo. I had seen so many people I loved suffer so much; I just couldn't keep my mouth shut when it came to marital problems. I felt obligated to help my clients, even though I was sometimes a bit inelegant.

## NATHAN'S REALITY

So when Nathan came in the next week, I got his hair cut just enough that he couldn't leave my chair and then started in. "Wow, Sharon was really exhausted when she came in yesterday," I said. I was full of anticipation for his response.

"Really," Nathan said, somewhat surprised. "I haven't noticed anything."

"Well, you wouldn't," I said, trying to sound lighthearted and teasing. I knew, however, that the subject was crucial to his marriage. "You're a man, and men never notice any of those things."

What Nathan said next sent me reeling.

"I don't know why she's so tired," he said. "She doesn't do much around the house."

My perfect opportunity for some dialogue had just opened up, and I intended to take full advantage of it. I could see why Sharon didn't want to broach the subject. She'd have been completely insulted at the last statement and probably would have stormed away. That would have been the end of it, yet there was so much more to say.

"What does Sharon do in the house?" I asked, not knowing what the cad was going to say. Whatever it was, I knew I'd have ammunition.

"Nothing," Nathan answered. "Sometimes she leaves the dishes in the sink at night and then there's double to do the next day."

"So who does the double the next day?" I prodded.

"Well, she does when she finally gets around to it," Nathan said.

"So who makes the dinner that dirties the dishes?"

By now Nathan realized what was going on. "Well, she does," he said. "But sometimes the dinners are awful. You can tell she doesn't take much time."

I couldn't believe my ears.

I told Nathan I was going to force him to listen to my poem, "A Mother's Lament." As I read it, I kept looking at him to see if he was listening. "This is what mothers go though every day," I said. "It's not easy being a mother." Then I got more bold and asked him, "What do you do when you get home from work?"

He didn't have his haircut finished, or I think he would have been out of there.

"I'm tired when I get home," Nathan said. "I sit down and veg in front of the TV."

"And what does Sharon do when she gets home, after she picks up the kids from the babysitter?" I asked, hoping the last phrase I'd sneaked in would give him a clue. It didn't.

"I help her pick up the kids once in a while," Nathan said.

"Well, what does she do when she gets home?" I asked.

"She could veg too. She just doesn't want to."

"Did you just hear yourself?" I asked, exasperated. "Do you really think anyone would not want to rest when they got home?"

"Then why doesn't she?" Nathan asked. I think he really didn't know.

"Could it be because everybody is hungry, maybe the baby is screaming and needs attention, maybe the other two are fighting . . ." I was ready to continue, but Nathan had had enough.

"Okay, okay," he said. "I get it."

"The difference between you and Sharon is that you have a choice of what you're going to do when you get home," I said as though I was Nathan's mother. "Sharon doesn't have a choice." I tried to sound a little bit sheepish or loving because I knew I'd pushed him. "No wonder she's tired," I said.

"Well, I never even dreamed she was doing so much," Nathan said. "I see what you mean."

## "HELP" IS NOT BALANCE

Sharon called me in a week and said Nathan had been helping her out a little. "It drives me crazy," she said. "Every time he helps me a little, he wants to be thanked, and if I don't thank him, he thinks he shouldn't keep helping."

In our society, we have evolved in almost every area. We got stuck, however, regarding domesticity, and one sticky little four-letter word has held us back: HELP.

The following is a simplified history, but the general trend is accurate. In the early days, the men and boys in the family were out on the farm trying to eke out a living, usually from dusk until dawn. The women took care of the house, garden, food storage, sewing, and meals. All the women and girls would help with smaller children. Both men and women worked six days a week, took Sunday off, and everyone suffered collectively. It had to be extremely difficult in those days.

## 40 HOURS FOR HUSBANDS, 24/7 FOR WIVES

As industrialization lured families into cities, men got a forty- or fifty-hour work week, and women stayed home and took care of the children and the house seven days a week. The woman's job was still very much like it had been on the farm: she was responsible for the house, garden, canning, meals, and smaller children. While machines had made tasks like washing clothes a bit easier, all the clothes still had to be washed, and the machines had to be maintained. Bills now had to be paid. Vacations had to be planned, and packing had to be done. That hallmark of prosperity, the flower garden, now had to be planted, weeded, and watered. Everyone still assumed that any work that went on in the home belonged to the woman, and her workweek always included the graveyard shift, overtime, and holidays.

## ONLY SUPERWOMEN NEED APPLY

When women wanted or had to work outside the home, they had to adopt the Superwoman stance because opposition to their working was so great. Like me, many women had to prove they could do it all if they wanted to have a career. And this was okay as long as there were no children, but when the children came along, it was almost unbearable. As far as the husbands knew, their wives were doing it all and making it look easy, so how difficult could it be? Women who chose to be full-time homemakers had it no easier because society hadn't come to appreciate the constant work that housekeeping and child-raising entail.

Household jobs had become unbalanced. Everything outside of breadwinning was expected to be done by the wife, and the workload was just enormous. The unfairness caused resentment.

So today we have wives with two jobs—one at work and the other at home. Her responsibilities at home now go far beyond keeping up a nice little house and feeding her family. We now have schools farther from home, dance lessons, sports, Scouts, music lessons, and more. With each child's activity, there are clothes to wash, practices to attend, and competitions to travel to. Each and every activity requires someone to be the driver. We have bigger houses to take care of and more recreational toys. Even our paperwork is more complex now that we have to manage our 401(k) and IRA accounts, invest wisely, budget, and get the best possible rate on fifty-seven kinds of insurance.

The problem of men going through life unaware of the ever-growing amount of work to do at home has profound consequences: women carry around anger, resentment, feelings of failure, frustration, and depression, and sometimes they finally explode. When they do, it often ends in divorce.

## THE IDEA OF "HELP"

Over the decades as this predicament evolved, we slowly began to realize that men should at least "help." We believe the husband should "help" the wife wash the dishes. Or a counselor encourages the husband to "help out your wife once in a while." This is very good advice, apart from the fact that we are using a vague word, asking for far too little, and assuming that all domestic stuff is women's work in the first place.

The missing link, the reason that we've evolved into women's lib—but never into male-female equality—is that "help" isn't helpful.

## ONE JOB FOR WOMEN ONLY

There is only one category of domestic responsibility that we in the modern world should assume is the woman's job and her job only: babies—pregnancy, giving birth, and breast-feeding. As much as some of us would like, medical advances stop short of men becoming pregnant. So of course, we never assume that these jobs would be a man's responsibilities, and it would be ridiculous to resent him for not offering to "help" with these.

## ALL OTHER JOBS AVAILABLE FOR SHARING

But we have no logical reason to believe that getting up with children in the middle of the night, changing diapers, washing clothes, buying groceries, cooking dinners, cleaning the cars, ironing, vacuuming, dusting, making beds, mowing lawns, planting flowers, weeding gardens, paying bills, washing windows, painting, spackling, wallpapering, packing for trips, unpacking after trips, loading and unloading the dishwasher, or washing dishes by hand—along with hundreds of other tasks—are women's jobs and that men could, as a kind gesture, occasionally offer help in doing them. These are the jobs of householders, and householders are the people who live in a house.

Therefore, whether it's your opinion that a woman should work full-time in an office or part-time in an office or full-time raising children at home, the jobs of householders should be shared equally among the householders. Women, men, and children over a certain age are all householders.

The illusion that men and children should occasionally "help" is flat-out wrong. "Help" is a favor you do for someone when it's convenient for you or if you feel like doing it. In the overwhelming challenge of raising kids and managing a household, "help" is an inadequate injunction, a dirty four-letter word where "shared responsibility" should be taught instead.

This shift in perspective would finally make things fair. It would finally free women to have fun with their families, to watch football with their spouses, and to go to book clubs with their girlfriends. But the purpose of the shift is not just to make things fair. It is the only way to keep marriages together in a world where people can and do get divorced when they feel dissatisfied. More young men and women are opting out, leaving toddlers to be raised by stepparents and forcing them to be shuffled back and forth.

## TOXIC IMBALANCE

If it were the overwork alone that was causing high divorce rates, it wouldn't be such a problem, but the resentment, anger, and frustration that come with the work imbalance are far more toxic than physical labor, and these feelings are the real reasons women divorce their husbands.

I see more and more news reports and talk shows in which wives complain that they just can't get cooperation from their husbands on the domestic front. That dirty word "help" is thrown around, but nobody finds a solution. On a 2002 episode of "Good Morning America," sixteen couples were asked what caused the most contention in their marriages. The answer was not sex nor money nor in-laws. They all said the most fights and dissatisfaction arose over husbands not "helping" at home and that if they did "help," they did it poorly and had to be told constantly what to do.

Most men have absolutely no idea what it takes to run a household, especially one with small children. Until a man has firsthand experience doing so, for longer than a weekend, he thinks it's a piece of cake.

## EXAMPLE OF ROOMMATES

When two young people are considering becoming roommates, they divide up the chores fairly or they both ignore any need for chores to be done at all. They ignore the dust bunnies under the beds, heap their clothes on the floors, and go out to eat.

Guess what happens when a man and woman become married roommates? They both automatically assume that the home will be the woman's responsibility, and it continues to be as the family grows and the job takes on new complexities.

## "SORRY, I HAVE A GOLF GAME"

We call a man a good husband if he will "help," and his help comes when he doesn't have a golf game planned, a buddy who wants to go fishing, extra work he brought home from the office, or when he's not too tired. When he does help, in most cases, he resents it and expects to be thanked because he believes he was assisting his wife with her responsibilities.

Men still believe this to be true, but now women know there is something wrong with this picture. And the gap in communication between the two is causing perfectly good couples to hate each other and divorce.

Who can we blame? Nobody. As author Anna Quindlen said, "It's not victim-hood, it's history."

## CHORES OF THEIR OWN

Husbands don't know what you want them to do in order to "help." If you tell them what to do, they forget very quickly, they critique your method, or they call you a nag. This is because they believe—and you believe and your children believe—that whatever job they are asked to do is not their job in the first place.

Husbands need the autonomy to do jobs themselves. Since the male brain works differently than the female brain, they need to do their jobs differently than women would do them. And they need to think the job they're doing is important, not just lowly women's work. So the jobs husbands do have to be their very own.

## SOME HARD ADVICE

Take a deep breath for this next advice. Consider relaxing your standards for work completed by others. When a man or housekeeper takes on a job, they might not do it the exact way you are used to doing it. Your man, especially, will do his tasks his way.

One of the chores in our negotiations I left totally to my husband was the yard. Although I had taken immense pride in the beauty I'd created, I realized during our division of tasks that I could relinquish my control to Gerald. If he did it poorly or infrequently, it wouldn't bug me as much as, say, unvacuumed rugs.

When the yard started looking neglected and my flower bed became a thing of the past, I ignored it completely. My friends reminded me that if I did the yard work even once, I would nullify our entire division of chores.

After what seemed an eternity, something spectacular happened. Gerald began taking pride in doing this chore. His manicured yard soon put mine to shame. He was increasingly proud of his project and loved it when people would call him up and ask for his advice.

A man won't ever want you to tell him how to do his householder work. He can only take on permanent responsibilities if he can be self-directed and take pride in what he accomplishes. You are not to be his mother or his teacher or his critic. Accept his choices. Accept it if he forgets to do a chore. Don't do it for him, and don't nag him. In the end, he will deal with his own failures and be proud of his own successes.

## REMINDERS

- Help is not helpful. Permanent, shared responsibility is.
- Men have absolutely no idea what it takes to run a household.
- We can't blame our husbands. We've participated in making them this way.
- Let men do their jobs their own way.
- Relax your standards when someone takes over your former jobs so that you can relax!

# 9

# BOTH MEN AND WOMEN NEED REEDUCATING

> We hold onto our old ideas, and they give us fuel to hate the mate we love.

**A**FTER I WENT ON strike and Gerald and I had agreed on our newly divided responsibilities, he would still say things like, "Did you see how I helped you with the basement/the yard/the garage?" But because the jobs we had designated for him had to be lifetime responsibilities in order for the system to work, I had to remind Gerald that cleaning the basement or yard or garage was not my job anymore. These were his jobs, and if I ever did these jobs, I would be helping him. In fact, when my job became less stressful and he had to take on longer hours at work, I began doing more to assist Gerald with his jobs, eventually hiring a cleaning lady once a week. That left very little for him to do regularly, but it also kept the enormous workload from falling back on me, now and later in our retirement.

## THE REWARDS OF BALANCE

The result of our division of labor was amazing. Gerald said it was a small price to pay not to have me mad at him all the time. We suddenly had more time together, more mutual respect, more compatibility on how to discipline the children, and, of course, a better sex life.

On one of Gerald's business trips to San Francisco, we were relaxing on the bed of our luxurious hotel room before going out to dinner and a night on the town with Gerald's colleagues.

"Do you realize this is the first of all our trips to San Francisco you haven't been so exhausted we couldn't have fun?" Gerald said. He hugged me tightly. "You don't know how good this feels."

That was the story of our life poststrike. Before my family started to cooperate on householder chores, I would work for three days to make sure I left my house immaculate before I went on a trip. On the trip, I would be exhausted and ruin everyone's fun by insisting on ending the evening early. Gerald actually started to wait until the last minute to let me know about a trip so I wouldn't go gangbusters on the house. It didn't work. I would stay up all night if I had to.

Now we were on a trip that we were both enjoying. The cooperation I was getting at home made it unnecessary to rush at the last minute. I have to say, I couldn't believe how much fun I could have in San Francisco when I wasn't catatonic.

## DESERVING OF RESPECT

I also discovered, to my surprise, that more important than the love that came as a result of my strike, Gerald had also found a healthy new respect for me that had been missing for a lot of years. I grant that it would be a little difficult to respect someone who was whining all the time, was angry at every turn, and didn't have enough self-confidence to demand being treated as an equal!

I realized through the strike process that I do deserve respect.

## "MY WORK"

We women have to educate ourselves. We are still hard-wired culturally to expect to do all the householder work. We still expect to keep the house in perfect shape all by ourselves, even if we have small children and even if we have a full-time job. Our whole identity has been wrapped up in whether we are good enough mothers and good enough wives. The ugly little secret is that we want it this way. We don't want to have to ask for change. We don't want to have to create change. We don't want to go through the discomfort of change. It's easier, we believe, to overwork ourselves and to continue to resent our husbands and kids for it.

Surprising as it may seem, as soon as a wife believes beyond a doubt that she most certainly isn't responsible for all the work in the house, it is easy to convince her husband. Believing in the balance of householder chores, however, also requires not worrying about what your neighbor thinks, what your best friend thinks, or what your mother-in-law thinks. Believing it requires not caring what anyone else thinks.

## JENNY PROTESTS BOTH WAYS

One day I had my client Jenny in my chair and we were discussing how unfair it is that she works and does all the housework while her husband has all the free time a forty-hour-a-week job gives him. The conversation changed noticeably, however, when another client, Bonnie, left the salon.

"I used to live by Bonnie," Jenny informed me. With disgust in her voice, she added, "Do you know she used to have a housekeeper?"

"Really," I baited her. "That's awful!"

"I know," Jenny said. "She couldn't even do her own work."

Well, I knew I had her, so I swung Jenny around in her chair and asked, "Are you really listening to yourself? You have been so angry for years because Tom never helps you and you can't do it all." Slowly and purposefully I said, "Maybe that's what you need, someone to come in and clean for you once a week."

Jenny was horrified. "I could never do that," she said. "What would people think? I couldn't have anyone else do my work."

"Your work?" I asked with glee. "I thought you said it was half his work."

Jenny shut me right down. "Well, I can't afford it anyway," she said.

We hold onto our old ideas, and they give us fuel to hate the mate we love.

## HIRING A DOMESTIC SERVICE

"We quibble in our minds as to whether domestic help is an unnecessary luxury or a modern necessity," columnist Jeff Opdyke wrote in a 2007 *Wall Street Journal* article. "It seems to me quite archaic to still be of the mind-set that keeping your own house clean and tidy is part of life when two people in the house are working."

As a wife and mother, I would rather go without food for two days, cancel a night out for dinner, or opt not to have a new outfit before I would release the woman who helps me for three hours a week! Imagine: you could spend more time with your children. You could spend more time with your husband, going on walks or watching NASCAR, whatever is your interest, without worrying the whole time that you're leaving your chores undone.

Opdyke also experienced additional benefits within his family: He said his ten-year-old son was busy with extracurricular activities at school and that "his time is as squeezed as ours. If he has free time we want to play with him as a family. We don't want him to feel his days are a monotonous blur of work at school and more work at home. . . . Talking to friends sealed the deal for me. Though I still feel queasy hiring someone to manage a mess I think we should be managing ourselves, I recognize that we're only creating a level of unnecessary tension in our life. Really, Amy shouldn't take vacation time just to fold clothes. Neither of us should have to walk past the laundry room feeling guilty for ignoring that mountain because we have another cliff to scale first."

I always thank my housekeeper. I couldn't tend my grandkids on my two days off if I didn't have her. I couldn't take off with Gerald on a moment's notice either. And what an aphrodisiac that is!

## BACKLASH TO WOMEN'S LIBERATION

Men, sadly, have a warped view of the woman's world, and we women haven't helped that one bit. Even feminism has hurt our cause. The fight for women's rights has made many more things possible for women, but like all good ideas, it has had some major negative fallout. The movement left a lot of men with the idea that they have to fight for their maleness. It has made them assume that everything is lopsided in the woman's favor, which it isn't. We may have to get over the resentment men have for women's lib before we can even let men know that we need their cooperation.

In my industrial town, for example, men spout off against women who work as underground coal miners at the same rate of pay but have to let the men do the real muscle-busting work. I have no idea what really goes on underground, but this is the diatribe I have heard from many of my male clients, and they bring their assumptions and resentment home with them to their wives.

Consider this letter to the editor I found in the *Salt Lake Tribune*:

> At last I can applaud an editorial of the *Tribune*—about the equal rights amendment and the tyranny of the ERA rhetoric.
>
> Women have used tears and shouts and nagging to get everything for a long time now and I'm glad the *Tribune* finally got fed up. The good life for women includes living longer than men, enjoying

childbearing and child-rearing, and working for nice guys at good jobs paying at least minimum wage, and often a few pennies more. There are other benefits, too, like doing easy household chores (and leaving lawn work to men).

Still, women are not satisfied. They demand ERA, but are they equal? Women aren't tall. They aren't strong, and can't box. They paint their faces every morning to look healthy but still they get frequent headaches, usually around bedtime.

Why give equal rights to such unequal people?

And ask yourself when was the last time your girlfriend picked up the tab on a date? Mine hasn't and what's equal about that?

I am proud of my maleness. Bad enough we gave civil rights to those protesting minorities of the 1960s. If we do the same now for the various Misses, Ms., and Mrs., hardly anyone will be around for us guys to be better than. Just kids, and they're no fun. The *Tribune* deserves praise for allowing men to finally get a word in edgewise over the tyranny of the lesser gender.

—Name Withheld
*Salt Lake Tribune*

I believe that letter is a joke, but some men really do feel that way.

Women cannot fuss about this situation. We cannot scream, nag, yell, or feel sorry for ourselves. If we want equality, we cannot make ourselves look like victims in the eyes of men who already resent the equality movement. The only solution to finding common ground with these men is to be strong and expect that you'll get results. In fact, make your results happen. First, you have to rid your mind of the generational consensus that has been embedded in our culture and our psyches that women should be able to do it all. Second, you have to love yourself enough that you know for a fact that you deserve more. Third, you must love yourself enough that society's mindless and outdated philosophy concerning householder work won't even phase you. And finally, you have to love your marriage and spouse enough that all the negativity by well-meaning folks will mean nothing because your spouse, marriage, and children will be worth it.

**REMINDERS**

- Keep open to learning—about yourself, especially—after your balancing action or strike.
- Love and respect can bloom after balancing householder chores. And you will have a newfound respect for yourself.
- Don't worry what the neighbor thinks or your best friend or your mother-in-law.
- Consider hiring a housekeeper if time and funds allow.

# 10

# THE REAL COST OF DIVORCE

> If happiness were the standard for judging a marriage, divorce would be justified in the average marriage once a day.

**M**Y FIVE O'CLOCK APPOINTMENT was twenty minutes late, and I was about ready to start cleaning up for the day, when all of a sudden the door swung open and, one right after another, three toddlers scrambled in. They were three beautiful girls, but their messy hair and clothes made them seem like they'd just tumbled out of bed. Their mother came behind them, helping an elderly woman through the door: my five o'clock.

The young woman told the children to sit down while she guided Grandma to my chair. I probably shouldn't have, but I laughed inside because I knew the young woman's demands would be fruitless. Sure enough, before she got Grandma into the chair, her tiniest girl had scattered all the magazines and pamphlets on the floor. To her credit, it looked like she was now about to construct the Eiffel Tower with them.

The middle child had found my remote control and was flipping through the TV channels. I hoped she'd land on an episode of Dr. Phil. The oldest child, no more than five, was the one trying to keep the younger two under control while her mother finally got the wobbly and half-deaf Grandma settled. When she saw the mess her children had already made, she didn't seem surprised—just humiliated and sorry.

I had never met the young woman before, but I found out that her name was Vikki and that she was the daughter-in-law of Rose, my new client from the assisted living center. I smiled at Vikki and said, "It's so difficult to be the mother of small children."

Her reply made me tingle with the fondest and most frustrated of memories. "It's the hardest job you'll ever love."

"How old is your littlest one?" I asked as I began to work on Grandma's hair.

The baby held one finger up on her right hand and used her chubby little left hand to hold the other four digits down. We both laughed at the wonder of this child.

"I also have a sixteen-year-old and a seventeen-year-old," Vikki offered without being nudged. "Two teenagers and three little ones, now that's a challenge."

I knew from experience that an age-range like that had likely happened because of divorce and remarriage. I listened with bated breath. Would she be any happier now?

## REBELLION AGAINST STEPDAD

"We're having all kinds of problems with the oldest one. Tommy wants to move out. He's been staying with one friend or another. He just doesn't want to be home," Vikki said. Her willingness to tell me everything didn't surprise me a bit. Once a woman gets going on family problems, she needs a good listener.

"You see," she continued, "he and his stepfather have never gotten along. They're both very stubborn."

On went the all-too-familiar monologue as Vikki picked magazines and papers off the floor for the fourth time. "Tommy never did forgive me for taking away his dad. And then forcing another one on him."

As I was putting Grandma under the dryer, the children were alternately shouting, arguing, and hanging from the light fixtures. I got the sense that this was what Vikki went through every day. No wonder she wanted someone to talk to. "How does he feel about his real dad?" I asked.

"He really loves his dad," Vikki said. "And his dad has no idea about all the problems we've had. We're actually talking about sending Tommy to live with him, but his new wife doesn't like Tommy, and the feeling is mutual."

Then she said it, the thing I had known was coming.

## TRADING ONE PROBLEM FOR ... THE SAME

"My first husband is a great guy, he just never helped me when we were married. He was like having a third child," Vikki said. "I couldn't take it, so I left."

"And your second husband?"

"He's worse than the first one," Vikki whispered, aware that little ears were nearby. "Now I have no help. Plus my boys are miserable."

When Grandma's hair was done, Vikki went around the salon fixing all the calamities her toddlers had created. She adjusted the thermostat, stacked the magazines, and lowered the chairs before leading Grandma out the door. I could do nothing more than send her off with a pat on the back and a prayer.

I wondered if Vikki didn't wish she had stayed with her first husband and worked things out.

Divorce is nothing to take lightly. It costs us financially and emotionally, and it costs our kids too. And sometimes during the extreme stress of the process, we make decisions that we will regret the rest of our lives. Current statistics show that the average duration of first marriages that end in divorce is less than eight years and that second marriages that end in divorce last, on average, eight years as well. And while statistics have it that 50 percent of all first marriages will end in divorce, 60 percent of all second marriages end in divorce. It's as if we keep whistling the same tune over and over but hope it will somehow—without our changing anything—one day come out sounding like a symphony.

## CHILDREN OF DIVORCE

Going through a divorce as a child has consequences too. Children with divorced parents are 50 percent more likely themselves to divorce than children from intact homes. Living in a fatherless home accounts for the majority of behavior problems, high school dropouts, youth in prison, teen pregnancies, and other catastrophes. Rebellious teens can escalate their resentment to crazy-making levels against stepparents and the person who took them away from their other biological parent.

The financial blows are hard too, for both you and your children. Divorced women suffer a 45 percent decrease in their standard of living after a divorce. Divorce proceedings take a year on average, but if a case actually goes before a judge to resolve differences over money or custody, litigation can take two years. Attorney fees run from 250 to 450 dollars an hour, and you will pay for every single phone call. The debt can cost each party as much as 60,000 dollars.

Some of my clients have started the divorce process trying to manage the details themselves or with a divorce mediator, especially when there was little property involved. Child support and child custody, however, always become the source of arguments, and I only encountered one woman who didn't finally get an attorney. She wanted out of the stress of the divorce so badly, she gave her ex-husband everything and regretted it her whole life.

Once we have children, we have to take the question of whether to divorce even more seriously. Children don't ask us to be born, and it's our obligation to raise them as a family until they are grown, if it is at all humanly possible. Granted, you should never stay in a marriage involving abuse, but relatively few women divorce on grounds that strong.

## DIVORCE AND DATING

One woman commented to me specifically about the post-divorce dating scene. "Who in their right mind would get wrapped up in a woman, no matter how much she has to offer, who has three kids waiting for her at home?" she asked. "That notion never crossed my mind when I was filing for divorce and looking for a better life."

Her ex, however, was able to move on more easily. He was free to date whomever he wanted because no "little eyes" were there to keep track of the women going in and out of the house. He could spend as much money as he wanted on dating and on the kids because he was the one who still had the good job. He spoiled the kids on the weekend and then sent them back home to ask Mom why she never took them on shopping sprees or to Disneyland.

## TAKING THE "EASY" WAY OUT

There are three main arguments that couples in average, workable relationships use to justify divorce:

1. If you're not happy in your marriage, it's not healthy for you to stay married, nor is it healthy for your children.
2. It's better for children to see their parents divorced than it is to see them together and fighting.
3. It's unhealthy for parents to stay together for the sake of the children.

What's a young mother to think when she hears this psycho-babble? It will lead her to a quick-fix divorce, and she'll have no idea of the quagmire she's getting herself and her children into for all their lifetimes. Any woman who uses one of those typical arguments in my salon will get an earful.

## ARGUMENT #1

Let's examine argument #1: If you're not happy in your marriage, it's not healthy for you to stay married, nor is it healthy for your children.

If happiness were the standard for judging a marriage, divorce would be justified in the average marriage once a day. Happiness is a human emotion, and the lack of it is not the reason to make a life-altering choice. The fact is, if you've ever been happy together, you can get happy again. Your children should not have to become unhappy in the future because you are unhappy now.

Just think, you loved your husband when you married him. Now you have children you adore. On paper that sounds better than happy; that sounds heavenly. But we all know that life is not a fairy tale and that anger and resentment build. Along with those angelic children come mountains of work and hardships.

To cope with the work and hardships, you try to come up with a solution. You think that even though your children require you to work and sacrifice, you would never kick them out because they are worth all the trouble. So let's kick out the husband instead. He seems to be the one causing all the problems. He doesn't help. He doesn't seem to think you do anything right. He is the reason that you not only have a truckload more work to do but also have an unwelcome critic looking over your shoulder as you try to get it done.

### Hey, I'd Get Rid of Him Too . . . or Would I?

**What if:** He doesn't have the faintest idea what he's doing wrong?

**What if:** When you complain, the only way he as a man knows how to help you is to show you a "better" way of doing things?

**What if:** Without him, 100 percent of all responsibilities will fall on you?

**What if:** He's still the same wonderful guy you fell in love with, but he doesn't know what to do for you?

If you are unhappy in your marriage, you can get happy again. The key is in discovering specifically what you want and then using a successful program to get it. Going to a marriage counselor is a great way to start. If you can't get your husband to go to a counselor, go by yourself. He may follow. If he doesn't, you will still get your fill of new life skills, and you'll be able to use these in the relationship to fix and avoid problems you would have fallen into in the past.

## ARGUMENT #2

Now let's examine argument #2: It's better for children to see parents divorced than to see them fighting all the time.

How ridiculous is that, really? Chances are, if you are fighting all the time while you're married, you will continue to fight after the divorce. Only then you will be fighting over the children. Will the children later see divorce as the answer to any fight and want to leave you as they struggle through the teenage years?

According to clinical psychologist Dr. Liz Hale, there may not be such a thing as a good divorce. "Sure, we will all move on," she writes in an article, "but to what degree does the sting of divorce remain for all involved? Divorce requires children to exist somewhere between two homes. Whenever I speak to adult children of divorce, certain key phrases are repeated: My loyalties were always split; I never knew where I fit in; I was always saying good-bye to one of my parents; or I had to be a little adult dealing with grown-up issues."

### Lessons Learned by Children

Children who come from divorced families, like my client John's case below, have a higher likelihood of divorcing. Maybe divorce teaches children that problems can't be solved.

One afternoon, John came into the salon after a huge battle with his wife and stated that he was quitting his job and going to Denver.

"What's in Denver?" I asked.

"Nothing," he said. "I just thought Denver would be a good place for a new start."

He was talking like a teenage kid heading to college.

"Aren't you going to try and work on your marriage?" I asked as I doused him with the spray bottle.

"She drives me nuts," he said. "I'd just as soon find somebody else."

I almost dropped my scissors. How could anyone talk so casually about ending their marriage? I couldn't let this go on in my salon.

I asked, "What is it about her that drives you crazy?"

John gave a reply I'd heard from all my other male clients: meals were sporadic, the house wasn't clean, and his wife constantly nagged him for help. When he finished with his list, I let John know that he wasn't going to find a woman who wasn't like that, especially if he didn't do his part.

"Aw, come on, Sherri," he said. He left, but our conversation must have opened his eyes because that Saturday he and his wife both visited me at the salon after hours to discuss the ups and downs of marriage.

I bullied the two of them into going to a marriage counselor. It started out rough but eventually gave them both a new outlook on marriage. After a year or so, John told me he was so thankful he still had his wife and little girl. "I used to think I would probably be married two or three times like my mom," he said. "I even got married with the idea that if it didn't work out I could just get divorced." His mother is now on her fourth husband who is a drinker.

How many children of divorce think the same way? We all internalize what we see growing up, and we rely on our childhood interpretations of life to inform our choices as adults. If we grow up seeing parents or close friends divorce, we think that our relationships will eventually end that way too. Children can't see the real cost of divorce, truly understand the quality of their parents' lives after they've gone through divorce, or see the quality of others' lives who have worked out differences and remained together instead.

## ARGUMENT #3

Now let's examine argument #3: Parents should not stay together just for the sake of the children.

In the first place, anything parents do for the sake of the children is wonderful! More wonderful still would be not to force a child to be shifted back and forth. Nor to force him to travel out of town because the court says he should. Nor to force stepparents and stepsiblings on him every time a remarriage occurs. Nor to force him into court to solve your problems.

After all of these arguments and their "real-life" flaws, the original marriage seems like the place to be. In almost every situation, no stepfather will love your children as much as their own dad does. I certainly don't want to take anything away from the stepfathers who have been wonderful and loving to their stepchildren, but from what I hear from my clients, those fantastic examples are few and far between.

## Fix, Not Flee, an Unhappy Marriage

You should not stay in an unhappy marriage for the sake of the children. You should fix your unhappy marriage for the sake of the children and everyone else. Happiness is a feeling, and feelings can be restored. Staying in what Liz Hale calls a "good-enough marriage" is better than a divorce. For the sake of the children, there is nothing better than to show them not to give up and to work through their unhappiness until it turns to happiness. There is nothing better than showing your kids that having a lifelong relationship is possible for you and for them.

And staying together just until the kids are out of the house is cheating. Adult children still learn by your example, and a divorce will still confuse them. It will still hurt them. It will still make them question their own level of commitment in relationships. It will still force them to deal with stepparents, and it will force their children to deal with stepgrandparents, some of whom just might not like them.

## THE POWER OF A WISE COUNSELOR

One thing I have discovered is that communication is automatic when you're in therapy. Sometimes it's not very comfortable in the beginning because all the negative feelings are bubbling out from both parties. All of this is happening, however, in a safe environment, and both parties promise to return. There's no bolting from the therapist's office because one person doesn't like what he or she hears. Therapy forces communication.

I have talked to many couples who have had ups and downs and long periods of time when they didn't even like each other. But once they learned to skillfully work through their problems, for the sake of their children and for their own sakes, they ended up with happy marriages again. Moreover, their lives were far better than those of their divorced friends. They had a sense of security in one another, had solid finances, and could easily grow into being grandparents of their own children's children.

Their divorced friends spent their time fighting with ex-spouses over who could get a weekend with the grandchildren. They quibbled with second (or third) spouses over whose set of grandchildren it was more important to see this holiday or this month and tried to explain to their own grandchildren why Grandma and Grandpa couldn't come visit together.

The couples who stayed together and worked on their marriages, however, are having the time of their lives with their grandchildren. Neither grandparent has to pretend to enjoy kids he or she doesn't know—they both worship the same group of children. This brings a certain ease and joy to their lives, and it makes life easier for the kids too. This is their reward for making their relationship work—a reward that surpasses all of their expectations.

## REMINDERS

- Don't get rid of one man who doesn't take responsibility only to attract another who doesn't take responsibility.
- Children who live without their fathers experience the highest rates of behavioral problems, high school dropouts, teen pregnancies, and youth in prison.
- After a divorce, women suffer a 45 percent decrease in their standard of living.
- The three main reasons popular culture uses to justify divorce are wrong, wrong, wrong.
- Therapy is cheaper and easier than divorce.

# 11

# THE RULE OF THE RULER;

## OR, WHY SHOULD I STAY WITH THIS JERK?

> When we trade in one man for another, we are trading one man's set of faults for another man's set of faults. Often we dwell on our husband's shortcomings and compare those with another man's good points rather than comparing the faults of both.

**S**HELLY WAS A CLIENT from out of town who was married to a prominent attorney. She had been coming to me for eighteen years, and in that time, although I had never met her husband, I felt like I knew him and their six children. They were all she talked about, and their life together seemed ideal. He was involved in the children's everyday lives, school functions, Scout excursions, and church activities. Practically everything they did, they did as a family.

Then after I had heard nothing but great things, one day Shelly came into my salon, white-faced and with shoulders down. I knew that something was dreadfully wrong. "What's the matter?" I said softly as I guided her to my chair.

She began to cry. "My marriage is over," she said between sobs.

Just like that.

"I caught him with another woman," she said.

That statement sent me reeling. The saint of twenty years had smashed both our bubbles.

"He acts like he wants out," she said. "He even told me this isn't the first time."

I couldn't help now but to read between the lines of their ideal life. Shelly's husband had every opportunity to meet beautiful women; he was out of town a lot for work, so there would be no reason to ever suspect he was up to something. And, although he was involved with the children, there was still the problem of imbalanced householder work. Shelly was the one who was busy all of the time and was probably too exhausted to even wonder if anything so devastating had been going on. She was too busy with her six children to keep herself looking sexy, and she was in the midst of marital burnout.

## IN NO SHAPE TO MAKE LIFE-ALTERING DECISIONS

While she was getting her hair done, we talked and talked about the situation. The only solution she could think of was to kick her husband out and file for divorce.

At this stage in our friendship and in my own "life research," I was completely unwilling to mind my own business and let Shelly go through with that knee-jerk plan. I could see what would come of it. Besides, here was a woman who was so hurt and so immobilized that she was in no shape to make a life-altering decision. Try as I did, though, I couldn't kindly talk her out of it. So I got testy and told her I wouldn't finish her hair or even let her out of my chair until she promised she would not file for divorce. I knew if she left, I wouldn't see her again until after the whole thing was over because she lived so far away.

"Do you want that little trollop moving in with your husband?" I asked with vigor.

"No," she answered.

"Okay!" I said, ever the tyrant. "I'll tell you what. If you still want to leave that jerk a month from now, have at it, but you are in no condition to make any decisions today."

"Well," Shelly said. "What can I do? He's the one who wants out." I could see the pain all over her face.

"So what!" I raged. "You let him know in no uncertain terms that it is your house too, your kids, your money, and that if he wants out, he is going to pay."

## TIME OUT

The idea was certainly not to forgive the man right now. It was to give Shelly some time to cool off and think logically. I knew from years of listening to her that her husband was definitely a good man and an A-plus father but that somewhere in the bottom half of his anatomy, something else was in charge, and I hoped that it was only temporary. I had a feeling that he may be a keeper in the long run, especially since I had seen divorce after divorce ruin my clients' lives.

I also knew that in Shelly's present state, she could see absolutely no good in her marriage. That would come after she had kicked her husband out and she could see him living with another woman. Then it would be too late.

So I canceled a few appointments, and we spent hours and hours making plans. Shelly would not be kicking her husband out, but he might wish at times that she had.

## THE CONSEQUENCES

This situation happened eight years ago, and the heartfelt concessions Shelly's husband made in order to keep Shelly and their girls—and his own self-respect—were quite impressive. He put all their assets in Shelly's name so she would be protected in case his belt ever came loose again. He agreed to therapy, and together they worked through the mutual problems that resulted in his cheating. Although it was a struggle, his changes provided a delightful jump start to the rest of their lives. Shelly learned to think of herself more. She learned to take time off, even from domestic work, and not to work herself to raggedness. Now she travels out of town with her husband, and their marriage is doing better than ever. Their girls are grown and doing well, and Shelly and her husband are deliriously happy as they enjoy their grandkids.

We shouldn't blame ourselves for our husbands' cheating, but we shouldn't automatically dump them for it when our lack of effective communication is partly to blame. It would surely cut down on the odds of infidelity if a husband didn't have double the free time his wife has. Balancing the householder work would change this dramatically. No longer would the man necessarily have a dowdy wife (one who has no time to fix herself up), a boring or uncooperative wife (one who is too tired to think of having fun), or an angry and resentful wife (for all the above reasons). None of these are attractive for anyone to come home to.

If we never communicate effectively about the situation of

householder overwork, we are sure to repeat it with husband after husband (see chapter 13). When we don't know how to fix the problem, it will follow us into the next relationship. It makes more sense to keep the relationship we have and fix the problem now.

I'm reminded of a phone call I got from another spurned wife whose husband had cheated on her. As soon as she heard my voice, she screeched into the phone, "Now tell me again why I'm supposed to stay with this jerk?"

Why? The reason is that I've seen hundreds of wives over lifetimes who, upon learning of infidelities, dumped their husbands prematurely and were sorry later. One client's "I'm outta here" attitude prevailed through five divorces. Now at 59, she is completely alone. She's still looking for the relationship she will never find because perfection is pretty hard to come by in a human being, even herself.

## THE RULE OF THE RULER

How did I know that Shelly should try to work it out with her husband? I used the Rule of the Ruler. Imagine using a ruler as a guide to your man's worth. If you measured his good qualities with a ruler and then you measured his faults, which "stack" would be taller? In Shelly's case, her husband was handsome, he was hardworking, he brought home a lot of money, and he spent a lot of time with his kids. Since I was outside the relationship, I didn't even know the hundred other wonderful things he did—the reasons she fell in love with him—but I could tell from years of talking to Shelly that they were there.

## TRY THE RULER EXERCISE YOURSELF

To begin the ruler exercise, get a 3x5 card or sheet of paper and list all your husband's good qualities on it. List everything, no matter how small. Is he hardworking? Is he handsome? Does he make you laugh? Does he love your children? Does he keep himself clean? Is he always on time? Does he keep his word? The card I wrote for my husband had twenty-two specific attributes that made me realize he was a definite keeper, no matter how enraged I often felt.

Remember, when we trade in one man for another, we are trading one man's set of faults for another man's set of faults. Often we dwell on our husband's shortcomings and compare those with another man's good points rather than comparing the faults of both. Chances are, a second husband's faults could very well include that he dislikes your children.

## TIME TO REVIEW THE CARD

When it seems like your husband is a gigantic jerk, take out the card and read it. If you have been honest with yourself and written down all of his good qualities, reading your card should pull you back to reality. In these moments, you can realize how fortunate you are.

This is a point often missed by divorcing women and men. Instead of focusing on the positives, we often waste so much time trying to change things about the people we love. These things are sometimes impossible to change, and they're often the things we loved about our partner when we met. So while you may wish that your husband were more romantic, you might have fallen in love with him because he is practical. These are two sides of the same coin. And from what I've seen, if you do find a hopeless romantic, more often than not he'll be romantic 100 percent of the time. When you aren't around, he might be hopelessly romancing someone else. Even your fantasy man can have his downsides.

I have the Serenity Prayer on a decorative card in the corner of my bathroom mirror. It says, "God, grant me the serenity to accept the things I cannot change, the courage to change the things I can, and the wisdom to know the difference." I apply the prayer to my husband every day because in my own heart, I really do know what I can and can't change about him.

## REMINDERS

- Remember why you loved your husband in the early days.
- You trade one man's faults for another man's faults.
- Accept imperfection. Perfection is difficult, even in yourself.
- There are some things you can and can't change in another person. Learn to know the difference.

# 12

# LET'S ANALYZE HIS FAULTS TOO

> "I'd like to make a motion that we face reality."
> —Bob Newhart, *The Bob Newhart Show*

**N**OW THAT YOU'VE SEPARATED your husband's good qualities from his faults, take a careful look at his faults too. If he criticizes the way you deal with the children or the condition of the house some days, take the time to remember when you were childless and you saw a friend's child in the midst of a temper tantrum or her house in chaos. Remember how inept you thought that parent was because you, in your infinite (childless) wisdom, thought you knew exactly how to handle everything. You were sure you'd never allow your child to scream like that or your bra to end up on the living room floor.

## DO HIS FAULTS COME FROM BEING CLUELESS?

Until you were thrust into the chaos of motherhood, you had no idea. Only then did you learn that the screaming, the vomiting, the clutter, and the toilet training mistakes are part of life. Only then did you learn that the events themselves become the boss. Your job becomes dealing with the events as they happen, not just preventing them.

Your husband might be stuck in this phase of infinite childless wisdom because he has never experienced full-time parenting and full-time housekeeping. He's not a jerk; it's just that from his uneducated point of view, he could do it so much better. Don't blame him. You've been there too, before your children thrust you into reality. To you, it's obvious—he's clueless. And he is, but he can't help it—not yet. Until men are forced to participate in everyday activities and to take care of children for more than twenty-four-hour stretches at a time, they will remain oblivious, no matter how caring, loving, and wonderful they are.

## SPOILED AND UNEDUCATED

Imagine yourself in his situation: You have a job to hold down and your wife is the householder, and maybe she has an outside job too. You have the freedom to come and go as you please, having done so from the beginning. Then, out of the blue, you have a nagging wife who insists she has too much to do and states that it's your responsibility as well as hers to handle the home front before you even think of going out to do something fun.

Would you automatically give up your freedom just because your wife is having a hard time and can't hold up her end of the bargain? If you were a man, you'd think of it like this, and you wouldn't see any benefit in giving up your fun. A husband is innocent in his belief—innocent as in unworldly and uneducated. No amount of nagging will help him break through it. What will fix the situation is your determination to help him learn in a way that makes him "get it." You have to do this skillfully. What's not going to fix the situation is dumping your husband and trying to find a man who is different. Once a husband actually understands what you are going through, the rest will take care of itself.

It is your responsibility to thrust this man into parenthood in the only way that finally made you get it, the only way that made you stop judging other mothers: your husband needs full-immersion therapy.

## FULL-IMMERSION THERAPY

Take a two- or three-day weekend off. Plan a trip, plan a family or friend's "emergency," or enroll in a seminar, and leave the kids with your husband. Make up an excuse if you have to. If your mother is your babysitter, let her know what you're up to so she'll be too busy to take the kids for him while you're away. Even better, take your mother-the-babysitter with you.

Carrie had been my client since she was thirteen. I'd gone through the teen years with her and a disastrous first marriage where physical violence, drugs, and a husband who wouldn't get a job were the realities. Carrie finally divorced and was terrified to get into another relationship, but after a few years she felt she'd found her soul mate.

I was ecstatic for Carrie. Don was everything her first husband was not, and he became a wonderful father to their three children. By the time the children came along, though, the problem of unbalanced householder work had been rearing its ugly head. Carrie had lived with worse and was very reluctant to rock the boat she was sailing on now, even though Don gave her a hard time about the condition of the house when he came home each night.

One day Carrie got a call from an aunt saying that her mother was sick and Carrie would have to fly out for a week. Don told her to go. He'd take a week off work and take care of the three little ones.

Carrie's big chance to balance the householder work had arrived. "Now, you don't have to say anything about this to Don," I said, "but once he takes care of everything by himself for a week, his whole attitude will change." I stressed to Carrie that the first day after she got home would be her only window of opportunity to divide the chores because Don would be in shock from the amount of work he'd handled at home.

Sure enough, he was. "I don't know how you do it all," he told Carrie when she arrived home. She delegated some chores to Don right then and there, and their already wonderful marriage hit a new high.

It wouldn't have worked if Don had had a babysitter to count on or a mother close by to take the kids. He had to experience the workload that Carrie had every day. Once he knew her situation for himself, he was willing to make things more fair.

## MY KIDS, MY KITCHEN=MY RESPONSIBILITY

Your husband's innocence may be as much of your own making as it has been his. Include him in the child-rearing, include him in everything domestic, and use the word "our" as much as possible.

One of the mistakes I made for years was to refer to the children as "my kids," the house as "my house," and the kitchen as "my kitchen." How could my husband take ownership when I made it clear in my language that these parts of the house, and even the children, were mine? If he ever did have an inclination to cook a meal, I had set him up to think, "I wouldn't want to mess up her kitchen." I excluded my husband from those parts of our life and then I resented him for not taking on any of their inherent responsibilities.

Just recently, my husband was watching three young women with their babies and toddlers, and he marveled at the joy emanating from those little ones. "You know," Gerald said, "I never got to experience that in our children, did I?"

"What neither of us realized," I said as I squeezed his hand, "is that while I was allowing you to be gone all the time and not insisting that you help with the kids, I was also robbing you of the wonder and magic that comes with those years, as hard as they sometimes are." I felt a surge of guilt. The joy I got from our little ones was so beyond explanation that I often think, "If I had any part of my life to live over, it would most certainly be that time when our children were little. No matter how hard it was, I would do it again in a heartbeat."

When we let our husbands escape the hardships, we automatically rob them of the thunderous *joy*.

## A BIRTHDAY TALE

I spent the first few years of my marriage waiting in anticipation for what Gerald was going to give me for my birthday, Mother's Day, and all the days that were supposed to prove how much he loved me.

The reality is, men forget about these things all the time just because they are men. Your husband is no worse than mine; most men don't care about holidays, presents, or romance. And if we play it the way we usually play it, we keep expecting the men to wake up and "get it" because as long as they don't, we can feel smug about it. We can keep resenting them and proving to ourselves that we're right and they're wrong, but we miss out on the love we really want.

I finally got smart.

After having quite a few letdowns, I decided that if holidays and presents were so important to me, I would just make Gerald remember them.

I began reminding him and our kids two weeks in advance that my birthday was coming and told them exactly what I wanted (a cream-colored, medium-sized sweater and a chocolate cake). I told them over and over again, excitedly and without nagging.

Not only was I pleased with the super event they created for me, but Gerald and the kids were all happy to be reminded that my birthday was coming, and they enjoyed planning for it. Each year they have continued to make a major event out of my birthday—because I stepped up and said specifically what I wanted even though that was really embarrassing. My adult children even travel from afar to celebrate as a family.

We all know the gifts aren't what really matter to us. It's what they represent: appreciation and love. So don't resent forgetfulness in any intimate situation; *make the celebration happen.*

## REMINDERS

- Remember why you loved your husband in the early days.
- Accept imperfection.
- Don't expect men (and children) to remember special dates. Don't be disappointed; instead, remind them in advance in a loving way.

# 13

# COMMUNICATE!

Suffering in silence only leads to more suffering.

**A**FTER I WENT ON STRIKE and my story had gone public, I had a man come up to me, congratulating me on what I'd done. Then he stated flatly, "You know, if my wife is stupid enough to do it all by herself, why should I help?"

My blood boiled at how callous he was, but I look back now and realize that we women are a bit like the man said.

I wouldn't call us stupid, but we do some dumb things. We suffer in silence, not wanting to hurt a husband's feelings, cause an argument, or maybe just not wanting to make his day any worse than his job has already made it.

What we don't realize is that when we suffer in silence, resentment, anger, and frustration begin to grow. They boil and stew inside us and erupt at all the wrong times. Even then, our anger never resolves the real issue.

## STRATEGIES THAT DON'T WORK AND USE UP TIME AND ENERGY

Poor communication often creates a type of temporary relief. It's a kind of instant gratification that ultimately harms our relationships, and it never gets our point across enough to make any changes. Such missed communication comes from the following:

*Angry outbursts*—This might get you some sympathy or it might get you a bigger fight. If you get sympathy, your husband will make you feel better in the moment, but nothing about your situation will change. If you get a bigger fight, you've gained nothing but a bigger fight. Either way, he seldom hears the words behind the anger.

*Crying*—This might cause your husband some guilt in the moment, but it will get you no results in the long run. The reason behind the crying becomes lost in his "there she goes again" reaction.

*Threats*—Threats, especially those made at the spur of the moment without considering (or being willing to act on) the consequences, become laughable and unbelievable as time passes. Your husband comes to know that you won't follow through with your threats, so he doesn't take them—or you—seriously.

*Running off in a huff (so your husband will have to do the work)*— Not only is a husband capable of doing all the householder work and then some for a short time, but he will also do the work better than you do it. He will prove once again that you are the one with the problem, and you will get no long-term relief.

*Nagging*—Not only does he not hear your words after the first few times, but he also resents someone constantly criticizing him or telling him what to do. He is less likely to do what you are asking when you repeat a request; in fact, he may resent you for asking him to do anything.

*Whining*—Don't complain about feeling sorry for yourself to your husband about something he does or doesn't do. There is nothing more unattractive to a man than a victim.

## STRATEGIES THAT DO WORK

Effective communication with men means thinking a bit like a man. They approach their communications differently than women do. Take time to really listen to and study your husband's technique for a while. Ultimately, you will find more success in your communications if you use the following strategies.

*Be strong, timely, and empathetic*—If you want a man to listen, you have to be strong and speak up when the need or issue arises. Effective communication expresses your need in a way that shows you respect and care about the other person.

*Lose the word "help"*—We've already noted that "I need you to help me more" are the seven most useless words in a woman's vocabulary. A man does not know what that means. The man wonders:

a. Does it mean help you do a single chore (like carry the groceries in)?

74

b. Does it mean follow you around, helping you do everything?

c. Does it mean something in between?

*Be specific and expect results*—State what you want specifically and kindly but with fortitude so he knows it's non-negotiable. For example, if you have reached the planning stage in a project or chore and you know exactly what you want, state it specifically. And state what you're going to do too so he has less room to object. "Honey," you might say, "I am behind in the ironing and I haven't got your clothes ready for tomorrow. Would you please iron your shirts while I finish the dishes, clean the kitchen, and get the kids ready for bed?" Most important, don't wait for an answer. Expect results. If the job doesn't get done, he will be responsible for his clothes not being ironed. That's not your problem, that's his.

## LIFE-CHANGING DIALOGUES

Instead of saying, "I just can't do all this by myself," make a life-changing dialogue. Try, "Honey, will you clear the dishes, put them in the dishwasher, and clean the kitchen while I help the kids with their homework and get their clothes ready for tomorrow?"

Or say, "Here are your clothes, Johnny. Go have your dad help you get dressed."

Or say, "Honey, I'm feeding the baby and getting him to sleep. Johnny and Mary need you to help them with their homework."

If by chance the husband says no, then you can say, "Okay, I'll trade you. You feed the baby and get him to sleep, and I'll help the kids with their homework." This may not work all the time, but if you handle the issue this way, over and over, you'll set a new standard. You'll also bring your husband's attention to how unfair your workload has been until now.

Unbalanced householder work is so entrenched in our society that there are no quick fixes, even going on strike. Because striking requires days, weeks, and sometimes months of preparation, any changes, even small, that you two can make now will start moving your relationship toward a true partnership.

## OK, ONE NAG: AVOID THE WRONG KIND OF COMMUNICATION

Beware of the usual method of communication—the wrong kind—where all your extra work finally gets to you and instead of stating that one fact calmly and clearly, you rant about everything else that's bothering you. It's understandable that letting issues build leads you to explode, but it is unproductive. Often such a conversation (or monologue) lets the real issue of overwork get muddled up by the rest of your complaints. The result is no progress.

If you have to sit your husband down and communicate your dissatisfaction in a frustrated or angry manner, be sure to state specifically what the problem is and why it makes you crazy. Keep focused on this subject alone.

## BEING RIGHT VERSUS BEING HAPPY

Do you remember why you loved your husband in the early days, the days when you were deeply in love? Do you remember the personality traits you loved about him? Do you remember when you first met what it was that made him stand out from other men?

Is it possible that since the marriage, your interactions with each other are what make everything difficult and not your partner's actions alone?

In a relationship, the memories of ugly arguments and disappointments are so vivid that these memories can crowd out happy, loving, delightful memories.

If you need to be right all the time, you will find yourself digging up and reviewing memories of each and every wrong thing your husband does. That way, in the midst of an argument, you can go to your memory bank, point to just the right wrongdoing, and win. Even if that wrongdoing happened weeks, months, or years ago.

Having to be right muddles your brain with so many angry memories that shout louder than and crowd out any others. You will be happier if you can reach that higher level in your relationship where being right isn't all that important. Then you can toss out the negative garbage in your brain to clear neural pathways to your treasures—the loving memories—so they are near the surface and the first to be remembered.

You are in charge of your own thoughts. When your thoughts get stuck on what's wrong instead of what's right, that leaves little room for the right kind of thinking—positive thinking.

Make sure that being right doesn't get in the way of getting results.

Reflect on how tiring it is for you to always have to be right and how that halts progress. If you both have to be right, then the bickering and the fighting will be never-ending. Yes, you can both feel powerful and beat your chests in victory over the other one, but is that what marriage is about? Have you solved anything by dealing with your problems in that way?

Your husband is the person whose friendship and love you wanted for the rest of your life. And he can still be that person unless you have to be right.

Train your brain to replace this negative form of communication with loving thoughts and strategies.

## LOVE AND BELIEVE IN YOURSELF!

The only way we can communicate successfully about our work overload is to know beyond a doubt that we shouldn't be responsible for all of the work in our household. We must know that our society has evolved in every other aspect and we must evolve here too.

Good communication comes about by being confident in what you want to convey. Communication is almost impossible when you believe one thing in your own mind but try to communicate a different message to your spouse. If you believe that you should be able to tackle wifehood, motherhood, outside work, and housework with ease, it will be difficult to say to your spouse, "I can't do this all by myself, and you have to share the householder chores."

It's better to train your brain to know beyond a doubt that you have a lot of worth, that you're not a slave to everyone's whims, that you can't be convinced that you must do it all, and that if you don't do it all you are not a failure.

Portray strength, and be resolute. Love yourself enough to care about what you think despite what anyone else thinks, and you'll be surprised how the lines of communication will open up. With them, your life will open up as well.

## PAPER COMMUNICATIONS

Sometimes you need an alternative to talking. Putting feelings in writing can be a solution. If you're a person who communicates better on paper, this will be a fruitful exercise for you. If your spouse is the quieter one, be sure to give him this option.

When you write a letter pointing out what you want to change in your relationship, be sure you insert some positive points. Here's an example:

Dear Henry,

I loved the way you complimented Tyson on his homework. It means so much to him when you're involved. I never dreamed how difficult it would be to work and then come home and cook, do dishes, get the kids ready for bed, and get their clothes ready for the morning. I am exhausted. I know you're tired too when you get home from work and enjoy sitting down and watching TV. That's why it means so much to me when I see you get involved with the kids' homework in the evening.

In the letter, give him a list of chores and say:

This is a list of chores I do all the time. I need you to pick out ten or fifteen of them that can be your responsibility from now on. I love you more than life itself, and this would help our relationship greatly.

This is just an example. What the letter does is lay your cards on the table. It allows your husband to know how you feel and for what reason, but not in an accusatory way. It lets him know the enormous workload you have, and it only asks him to pick ten or fifteen chores as his own.

Letting your husband pick his responsibilities makes them his choice—he is in charge of his own future. And if he balks at ten chores, ask him to pick five or perhaps three. Even a few chores permanently taken from your workload is a start.

## RELIGIOUS HIERARCHY

The need for communication is even greater in a situation where it seems to disappear: when husband and wife believe, for religious reasons, that the man should be the head of the household and that the woman should not question his decisions.

I'm not saying that it's wrong to believe this, but even in this situation, you have to communicate your desires and problems. You can do it respectfully. You can honor your husband even as you share your feelings with him. In fact, a husband of faith will benefit from this as much as a wife will.

I have talked with many people of such faith, and I know that resentment finds a fertile home here too. The husband whose wife can't communicate suffers. A lot. He suffers with her constant nagging, silent sadness, depression, or any other malady, including the effects of medications to "deal with" the unfair position of being overworked and underappreciated.

The solution is the same. You don't disrespect your husband. You don't undermine him to get your way. Instead, you do whatever it takes to make certain you are heard. This is not accomplished with screams, shouts, or demands. It is only accomplished with quiet, loving understanding and all the fortitude you can muster.

## MY DREAM

My dream is that in our near future, responsibility for householder work won't be an issue. Husbands and wives will divide the work evenly before they even get married. Society will realize that it must be this way out of necessity. A woman will never feel guilty for hiring a housekeeper nor for expecting her husband to do his own laundry. A man will never believe that making dinner is "her job" unless she's chosen that job for herself.

## REMINDERS

- Get rid of communication that doesn't work—angry outbursts, crying, threats, running off in a huff, nagging, and whining.
- Men communicate differently than women. Study your husband's technique.
- Be timely, strong, and empathetic.
- State your need specifically and expect results.
- Communicating on paper is an alternative to face-to-face communication.
- Is your need to be right getting in the way of your happiness?
- Women of patriarchal faith need to communicate their needs, for their sake and their husband's.

# 14

# STRIKE TEST

## HOW TO KNOW IF YOU REALLY NEED TO STRIKE

All the worries, all the headaches, all the planning, all the management, all the doing X, Y, and Z—are whose responsibility?

**S** EVERAL YEARS AGO, I traveled to Washington state—where my daughter, Nicole, was living—to attend a women's expo. At the time, I was curious whether women across the country felt as overworked as my clients did. And you know what? The feedback was identical.

Only two of the women who came to my booth said their husbands were awesome, sharing all the responsibilities. After two hours, one of those very women came back and said, "I thought I had better tell you, this is my third husband. I got rid of the ones who wouldn't help." Another lady stated that after having landed two duds, she now has a long-term boyfriend whom she refuses to marry. He actually still lets his mother take care of all his domestic stuff, and his girlfriend thinks that's as good as it can get. I thought that was a far cry from how the problem should be handled.

What really surprised me was that not one woman I talked to figured there was a way to solve the problem of household overwork. Two of them were actually planning divorces. In each woman's mind, it seemed easier to uproot her family and leave rather than to try to make a change in her existing household with her husband.

One of these women, Pam, was there with her mother-in-law. As we were discussing the domestic situation at Pam's house, the mother-in-law piped up and said, "Pam doesn't have to worry. She's got a wonderful husband. He helps her all the time."

An hour later, Pam came over by herself. She was seething. "That woman doesn't have a clue," she said. "What she doesn't realize is, I plan on filing for divorce this very week."

"Do you love your husband?" I asked.

"I can't even think about that," she said. She was irate. "I'm so sick of doing it all, I just don't care anymore."

None of this surprised me. Not her dilemma, nor her mother-in-law's impression of the situation. I had seen it all before.

"What if I could give you a way to make a change," I said as I took Pam by the arm. "You wouldn't have to leave."

She was resolute. "My three kids have been just as bad as Jerry," she said. "I'm leaving them too."

That thought made me sick. She said her children were eight, ten, and twelve. I thought, *Leaving my kids was the last thing I'd have done. My kids were my life.*

Pam would eventually feel the same way. I took her aside and explained the Fair Marriage Contract to her. I told her to try going on strike before she filed for divorce.

While my daughter was taking care of the other women clamoring around our booth, I spent time explaining to Pam that if she did decide to go on strike, she should under no circumstances jump the gun. I explained to her how important it was to prepare herself in order to get lasting results. I then gave her my daughter's phone number and told her to call me there in a couple of weeks.

Pam called me in a couple of days, which made me cringe because I knew she had jumped the gun.

She was excited and said that when faced with the contract and threats of a strike, her husband and three kids had given her a day off, had waited on her, and had promised to help more.

"Thank you so much," Pam said excitedly. "I never dreamed they would do all they did."

I hated to burst her bubble, but I knew she had just put a Band-Aid on a massive injury.

"What have they done today?" I asked. It was 5:00 p.m.

"Well, not much," she said. "But at least they know why I'm so mad."

It sounded like there had been no dialogue. Pam had expected her husband and kids to know instinctively what they were supposed to do.

I stressed that she needed to follow up immediately. "While they're still feeling bad for your overload," I instructed, "have all four of them pick at least three responsibilities from the list I gave you. These are things each of them will do around the house permanently. It is very important to get them to agree to this. And they will agree to it if you do it now."

There were fifty-two chores on the list I had given Pam. Fifty-two chores that had been hers exclusively. In order for each person to pick three chores, they'd have to read the whole list. Ask yourself, could someone look at the enormity of those tasks and not want to help? The guilt alone should do the trick.

"Then," I added, "there would be twelve whole chores subtracted from your regular responsibilities."

Pam said she'd do what I'd asked. She hung up the phone, still ecstatic.

This is one woman whose case I wish I had followed. She seemed to have a basically good family, and by the time I left Washington, she'd told me she'd changed her mind about the divorce and that she finally had some optimism.

I hope that it worked out for Pam, but she didn't go on a well-planned strike. She sacrificed much of the effectiveness and power that a strike can have, and since she wasn't prepared, she almost forgot the point of it all: to ask her husband and kids to take on permanent chores.

Recently I was discussing taking responsibility for four or five householder chores for a lifetime with a male client. He said, "That many chores? That's asking a lot." I replied, "Why? Your wife has fifty-two chores for a lifetime." I could tell by his face: he got it.

## STRIKE TEST

Before I tell you how to go on strike effectively, let's examine whether you need to go on full strike or if you could obtain your goals with a ministrike, for starters. A ministrike would be going away for a long weekend and arranging it so your husband would have to take care of the kids and the house without help. (And without him knowing you were up to anything.)

Ask yourself these questions:

1. Have I been married for over five years? (A newer marriage might benefit more readily from a ministrike since your habits aren't as set in concrete as those in an older marriage.)
2. Have I been doing every household duty by myself even after trying endlessly to receive help from my husband?
3. Does my husband have all the freedom for sports and activities while I have none?
4. Do I feel like a slave in my home?
5. Have I tried to get his attention (to no avail)?
6. Is my home free of domestic violence?
7. Am I seriously thinking about divorce?

The only way you can have a successful strike is if you answered "yes" to *all* of these questions. In that case, a full strike would be the most effective way for you to change your life. Skip the following information on ministrikes and continue to chapter 16 to learn how to launch an effective strike. I cannot say this enough, however: If your husband is violent or abusive, a strike is not appropriate.

## REMINDERS

- There are ways to change your householder workload instead of divorcing.
- If you strike, think it through. Don't get caught up in the euphoria of a moment of success.
- If you answered "yes" to all seven questions, a full strike would be the most effective way for you to change your life.
- A ministrike may serve those couples married less than five years.
- If your husband is violent or abusive, a strike is not appropriate.

# 15

# MINISTRIKE

## WEEKEND IMMERSION THERAPY

> "I stood awhile telling myself that no one could do all that. Slowly I saw that she was doing it."

**I**F THERE'S A CHANCE that a weekend away would do the trick, here's how to prepare yourself for success:

1. Make a plan to go away for the weekend without the kids. Plan to go somewhere that you can't easily come home from or promise yourself that you won't.

2. Let the person who often helps with your kids know what's going on so she won't jump in and help your husband. If the person is his mother and you have a good relationship, confide in her and let her know how dire your situation is. Plead with her to trust her own son to love his kids enough to take care of things while you're gone, and let her know about the outcome you expect.

3. Consider this a strike in your own mind, but don't tell your husband that. Let him think it's just a weekend away or an emergency in another city. If you tell him it's a strike, he'll do all the work better than you would have for the weekend just to prove how wimpy you are.

4. Copy the lists of chores at the back of this book and have them ready.

5. When you leave, tell your husband how wonderful it will be for him to bond with his kids. Tell him to call you with any problems.

6. When you are gone and he calls to complain, tell him how sorry you are because you know exactly what he's going through.

7. When you get back and he says he can't believe how much you do, be prepared with the list of the chores you do regularly. You could say something like, "While I was gone, I made a list of all I do. I was going to ask you to please share some of them with me. How about picking out fifteen of the chores that you'll always do? That would balance things out so much."

8. If you get back and he acts like it was a piece of cake, say, "Good. I'm so glad, because my sister wants me to go help her with her baby next week." Or this may be the time to pull out the contract and go on strike.

9. In most cases, make sure you have the list of chores ready immediately and wait until a later date to use the contract. The weekend isn't the time for the contract unless you're ready to tell your husband that the trip was planned for that purpose only.

## REMINDERS

- A weekend ministrike may be enough to awaken a young, naive husband to what "doing it all" means.
- Tell whoever often helps with your children the purpose of your weekend trip and ask them not to be available— or take them along!
- If your husband calls to complain, tell him how sorry you are because you know exactly what he's going through.
- Have the list of householder chores ready afterward for dividing.

# 16

# FULL STRIKE

## STEPS FOR SUCCESS

> Share everything: chores, love for each other, time for children, and most important, time to have a loving personal and sexual relationship with each other, free from resentment, anger, and despair.

**N**OW, IF YOU ANSWERED "yes" to all the questions in the strike test in chapter 14, you are a candidate for a complete strike to achieve a balance of householder chores with your husband and children.

To clear up any misconceptions you might have, here is what a strike is and what it isn't:

A strike *is* you making a dramatic stand on something you truly believe in—creating fair and balanced householder work that will improve your workload, your life, and your relationship with your husband. You must believe in the purpose of the strike so much that you're willing to do whatever it takes, for however long, to get results.

A strike *is not* one more game you play to get your way. It's not instant gratification. It's not a temporary fix. It's not a threat you make. If you are not certain that you will be able to go though with a strike, don't try it. A failed strike will leave you no chance to effectively strike again.

## IT'S NOT "A PIECE OF CAKE"

Before you begin your strike, you must do and know the things that Pam in our story in chapter 14 did not:

- You must be totally prepared and have a long-term plan in mind to help you stick it out because it will be tough.

- You must know what you are about to face. You might see a bigger mess in your house than you've ever lived with.

- You might experience letdowns, threats, and coercions from the people who love you. The children might rant about your motherly missteps. They might be embarrassed if your strike gets their friends' attention, and they might be angry that you've caused discomfort in the house.

- Keep your cool. Tell them that you love them and that this is the best possible thing you could do right now. But also keep your conversation short. Do not argue with your kids about the strike. Do not try to convince them that you're right. They are children, and even as teenagers, they won't understand householder work until they have households of their own.

- Your husband might threaten to leave because he doesn't want to put up with your shenanigans. This could be his way to get you to stop the strike and avoid additional householder work.

- Your husband might also try loving coercion to get you to end the strike. He might say that he's sorry and that he'll do better. He might promise that he'll start "helping" and that everything will be different. Everything cannot be different, however, until your husband experiences the workload and turmoil you go through daily. This will not happen in one day.

- A strike will take days. Your husband's promises to change, however genuine, will only produce more of the same in the long run. Then, if you've abandoned the strike due to his sweet promises, you'll be unable to strike again and have him take you seriously.

## DO NOT STRIKE IN A MARRIAGE WITH VIOLENCE

Once again, I cannot say this enough: I would never have attempted going on strike if I'd had a violent husband. I knew Gerald wasn't the type to hurt me, no matter how angry he got. Do not go on strike if you live in a violent situation. Get help.

## TEN STEPS TO A SUCCESSFUL STRIKE

1. First and foremost, keep your plan of going on strike a secret from everyone until you've read and internalized all the steps and are ready to act.

2. Read the entire Fair Marriage Contract and chore lists over once and then go over them again with your specific problems in mind. It might be that you have to get up at night with a newborn. You might be run ragged keeping up with toddlers. You might have loads and loads of extra laundry to do because of your husband's job and your kids' after-school activities. Thinking of these specific differences in your situation, go back over the contract and chore lists and revise them to suit your own situation.

3. Make sure that the wording on your contract is not the least bit evasive and that you and your family can follow it exactly. The householder chores must be listed in such a way that each family member can choose ownership of specific, individual chores. Each person becomes responsible permanently, not slipping back into occasionally "helping" you with "your responsibilities" again.

4. Get all the resentment and bad feelings behind you. Rid yourself of all thoughts of getting even with your husband and realize that the reason you haven't left him by now is because of your love and your determination to keep your family together. It will be that same love and determination that will carry you through this endeavor. If you need help to feel love for your husband at this point, turn to the "Rule of the Ruler" exercise.

5. Do not go about striking in a threatening or demanding way. Stay calm and polite. Keep in mind that your partner and your children have absolutely no idea what you're going through—they have never done it all themselves.

6. Ask yourself these questions, and answer truthfully:
   a. Am I prepared to follow the strike all the way through, no matter what the consequences?
   b. Am I prepared to put up with any difficulty for a short time—like stepping over messes, putting up with a husband or child's angry outbursts, or even getting an

earful from an in-law—in order to achieve results?

   c. Have I released all resentment, leaving me free to have a loving relationship throughout the strike?

7. It helps if you have a good friend who totally believes in what you are doing. Your friend can offer emotional support, but when the strike gets hard she can also remind you of the reasons you're doing it. She can remind you that it will be worth it and to hang in there.

8. Realize that you are in control. Physically and emotionally, your husband and children need you more than you need them. No matter how much they rant and rave over the strike, they are going to realize how much they need you when the strike is over. Not to mention, the longer the strike lasts, the more they are going to appreciate how much you do for them, and they'll be more aware of your past efforts. This will bring about an awareness, love, and respect from your family that you never thought possible.

9. Take the time to realize how important your role is and how much you have contributed to the household.

10. Have a backup plan. If things get unbearable, pack up and go visit your best friend or mother, without the kids, until an agreement is ready to be reached. Do not indulge in a shouting match.

## KEEP IN MIND—A STRIKE HALTED IN THE MIDDLE IS WORSE THAN NO STRIKE AT ALL

A few added thoughts: In advance, think carefully through any questions you think your family may ask and any real or faked misunderstandings about your strike they may throw at you. Write down your answers ahead of time to prevent any coercion, loss of temper, or any conversation that could lead to an argument or bad feelings on either part. This will keep you in total control.

## CHOOSING THE DAY TO STRIKE

Be absolutely sure you don't jump into a strike too soon. Pick your time. Pick your opportunity. Keep in mind that if this is done right, it can change your life. A few extra days of doing all the householder work now isn't going to make a difference.

When the day is right to go on strike, you might just sense it. A moment may just come up (as one did in my case) that makes you so angry you just know it's time.

Even though I went on strike spontaneously, my strike wasn't at all impulsive. I had my contract and chore list planned and printed out. I had a plan and a backup plan. I had thought through all the negatives in my head and was emotionally ready to survive the days it would take for a successful strike. So, even though I began the strike at the spur of the moment, it really wasn't on a whim. Do the same. Make sure every bit of the process is planned, and then whether you allow the moment to arise or decide to strike on a particular day, you can't go wrong.

## REPLACE ANGER WITH DETERMINATION

Once the strike has begun, anger cannot be part of the process, even if the moment that made you think "This is it!" was one that really made you angry. You will need to replace your anger with determination. And your determination will arise out of your knowledge that this is the best thing you could do for yourself and for your family.

You'll feel the determination to stay healthy. (Being a doormat doesn't constitute health.)

You'll feel the determination to get respect from your husband and children. (It's hard to respect a whiner who keeps doing the things she's whining about.)

You'll feel the determination to keep your marriage together and make it happier than ever. (Resentment stands in the way of happiness.)

Any other positive changes you can imagine coming out of the strike will fuel your determination too and help you keep the anger away.

## KEEP LOVE ALIVE

Another way to keep yourself in a loving attitude toward your husband is to get out the 3x5 card you made during the "Rule of the Ruler" exercise in chapter 11. Keep it handy. I keep mine in my recipe file. Take the card out and read it when it seems like he is a gigantic jerk and not worth keeping. And don't just read it, take the time to visualize how gentle your husband is with the kids or how strong he can be in a crisis. Remember how he shows up to work every day whether he wants to or not. Remember why you "knew" he was the one. Really imagine these things. Relive them. You'll feel your husband's qualities in your heart this way, and you'll start loving him more, even during your strike.

Remember again, in most cases, trading this man in for another would only be trading in his faults for another set of faults. And as universal as householder overwork is, you'd likely be trading a man who doesn't take responsibility for another man who . . . doesn't take responsibility.

## HOW LONG DO YOU STRIKE?

The strike should end when your husband is willing to read the contract and the list of chores aloud to you and the children and negotiate a change. If he does this unconvincingly or offers to sign the contract without reading it or without discussing it with the children, continue the strike.

Your husband's signature on the contract means nothing by itself. It's not a legal document, of course. Only understanding it all, having empathy for you and your workload, and willingly negotiating a change will make the contract work.

My strike went on for over a week. It was scary, but I figured the longer, the better. The more time my husband spent doing all my householder chores and taking care of the kids after putting in a full day at work, the more he would empathize with me. Because of the workload he'd be under, I can't imagine a husband dragging out a strike much longer than that. Any man with an ounce of sympathy would have to see the inequity of the situation and want to change it.

## IT'S ABOUT "TIME"

In this day and age, I'd like to think that nobody would have to take such drastic measures as I did. I would like to know that men would be at least aware of how unfair and unbalanced householder work is against their spouses. Some are. But even they don't know what to do about that. They want to be told specifically what to do, time and again, to make you happy. They think they're doing a wonderful job if they just help you out now and then. Secretly, I think they wish it would all just go away. So do I.

But until the laundry, the dishes, and the floors that need mopping just go away, consider a domestic strike. It's a great solution to this immense problem. The Fair Marriage Contract is a contract that you'll both understand, a contract that leaves nothing to the imagination.

Instead of arguing about who's doing what bit of work, you can snuggle up on the couch after the chores are done, knowing that their equal division has left time for you to be together. Without resentment. Without unfairness. Without guilt. Just love. Doesn't that sound worth it?

## REMINDERS

- Take time to plan your strike fully, including answers to questions or threats that may arise. Don't be impulsive.
- Keep your strike a secret from everyone until you are completely ready.
- Don't strike in anger, even if that prompts you to go on strike. Replace anger with love—you are doing this to keep your family together. Stay calm and be kind.
- Repeat to your family that you love them and that they are worth your strike action.
- Do not argue with your spouse or kids during the strike. Do not have long discussions. Let the strike, contract, and chore lists speak for themselves.

# 17

# THOUGHTS TO KEEP YOU STRONG AND SUSTAIN YOUR LOVE

> Seek first to understand, then to be understood.

**PHOTOCOPY THE FOLLOWING PAGES.** Keep them handy at all times during your strike as a reminder of why you are doing this when you feel yourself slipping. These thoughts worked for me. Sometimes I had to say them over and over to drown out the doubts or the angry words. *Patience.* That's another important thought. And *love.*

1. It's not on purpose. The probability that my husband or loved ones purposely put me in the impossible situation is practically zero.
2. Reread the card from the "Rule of the Ruler" exercise that lists all my husband's good traits.
3. Men are oblivious to our workload. Keep in mind that 95 percent of the male population is unaware of the intense problems a wife and mother faces. Men are oblivious to the weight of our daily responsibilities, even though we are doing it all right under their noses.
4. I loved my husband when we married. We can find love again through this process.
5. Remember the potential payoff. I will have my original husband, who can turn into an angel through this process. My children can live with their own father and mother in the same home—no custody fights, no stepparents. And later, my grandchildren will have the best grandpa and

grandma anyone could ever ask for.

6.  What I want most from my strike is a fairy tale come true: a lifetime of happiness with the man of my dreams—the man I first married.

7.  He will be worth the effort.

8.  I am worth the effort!

9.  We are worth it! It was this very thought that author Sherri Mills kept repeating and that made her determined to carry through her strike to the end. She said, "I constantly reinforced the idea to myself and to my family: we are worth saving."

10. Giving our children their own full-time dad is worth the effort.

11. Stay focused. Don't give in to gestures. Keep telling myself, "I've got to keep going. All my work cannot be for nothing. He will be worth the effort."

12. Mr. Clueless. He's not a jerk; it's just that from his uneducated point of view, he could do chores or child rearing so much better. Don't blame him. I've been there too, before our children thrust me into reality. To me, it's obvious—he is clueless. He is, but he can't help it, not yet. Until he is forced to participate in everyday activities and take care of the children 24/7, he will remain oblivious, no matter how caring, loving, and wonderful he is. That's why I'm striking.

13. My sanity and need for a balanced workload is worth the effort.

14. Hang in there. He's worth it. Remember not to get angry back at him. Stay loving and positive.

15. I can't get mad. I must stay strong. It's almost over. I've come this far. He's worth all the trouble.

16. Imagine myself in his position. I have a job to hold down and my wife is the householder, probably with an outside job too. I have the freedom to come and go as I please, having done so from the beginning of the marriage—and from childhood. Then, "out of the blue," I have a nagging wife who insists she has too much to do and states that it's my responsibility as well as hers to handle the home

front before I even think of going out to do something fun. Would I automatically give up my after-work freedom?

17. The bottom line is that staying with this man for a lifetime is certainly worth the effort. I will remind him that this is my ultimate reason for the strike and the contract.

18. I will tell him that I have the husband I want and I am willing to do whatever it takes to keep him.

19. The gift of "getting it." No amount of nagging will help him break through his cluelessness. What will fix the situation is my determination to help him learn in a way that makes him get it. It is my responsibility to thrust this man into parenthood and householder work in the only way that finally made me get it, the only way that made me stop judging other mothers: my husband needs full-immersion therapy.

20. Walking a mile in my shoes. When my husband actually understands what I am going through by doing it himself, the door will be opened for dramatic change and increased happiness.

21. Don't let his angry words or temper tantrum provoke me to anger. Stay calm. Stay loving. I am striking because I want to keep my family together.

22. Hang in there for sincerity. I won't allow my husband to sign the contract until I know that he has read the whole thing and understood it completely. I can tell if he is only halfhearted and just wants me off his case and wants this to end. If so, then he isn't sincere yet. All my work will be for nothing if I let him sign before he *really gets it*.

23. He must commit to the division of labor—in his heart—because he knows what I've been through. Because he's experienced it himself. Because he's walked a mile in my shoes.

24. After he's read the whole contract and empathetically understood it, he must meet with the kids and explain what their new roles will be. Then we can divide the chores permanently.

25. I must not let my children skip out on all householder work just as I let their father. This strike will set them on a

good, responsible path for their future happiness.

26. Author Sherri Mills's strong, masculine man started out the strike trying to prove he could do everything better than she had. Ultimately he realized what a monstrous endeavor that was. When he realized what she put up with day after day, he was horrified and even wanted to change the situation for her. In fact, he never even knew Sherri was suffering until she let him experience her workload for himself.

27. "Help" is a four-letter word. It's a favor one does for someone else when it's convenient. Or if one feels like doing it.

28. "Help" is not balance. It is not permanent. The job stays someone else's responsibility—mine. I am striking for permanent balance—for my husband to accept responsibility for his share of householder chores.

29. No turning back to settle for mere "help" around the house. Because if and when my husband did "help," he usually resented having to do it, had to be told again and again what to do, and expected to be thanked because he believed he was assisting me with *my* responsibility.

30. Our children should not have to become unhappy in the future because I am unhappy now.

31. This is my best hope for happiness. Unless I do something positive, there is a distinct possibility that our relationship will either slowly die because of nonaction (resulting in not caring) or suddenly explode in a devastating way because of my increasing resentment and deep hurt.

32. Solve the problem *now*. Until I learn how to solve the unbalanced householder workload in this marriage, I will take the same problem into any future relationships—and so will our children. And no future stepfather could love our children as much as their real father.

33. Hang onto the father of our children. Statistics show that we end up marrying the same type of person over and over. Why not hang on to the father of my children—the father who loves them a lot more than any stepfather could and whom the children love.

34. I expect to see rewards. My husband may say that his

chores are a small price to pay for not having me mad at him all the time.

35. Rewards of balance: More loving time together, more mutual respect, more compatibility on how to discipline the children, and, of course, a better sex life.

36. If I stay strong, I will have more quality time with my children and with my grandchildren. I will have more time to spend with my husband doing things we like to do together.

# 18

# THE WRONG WAY TO STRIKE

## A CASE STUDY

> A strike is *not* instant gratification. A strike *is* a well-thought-out plan using patience and, most of all, endurance. It's a life changer.

**C**YNTHIA WAS WRIGGLING AROUND in my chair as if she wanted to escape.

"Hold still," I said, "or I'll cut your ears off." I grabbed an ear and jokingly took a pretend snip.

"I'm just thinking about what I'm going to have for dinner," she muttered. She didn't seem to get the joke.

"As nervous as you are, one might think you're planning a meal for the Queen," I retorted, trying to keep the whole conversation comical. It didn't work. Cynthia knew if she didn't get home on time and have dinner on the table when her husband Allen got home from work, a war just might erupt.

Cynthia had been married to Allen for fifteen years, and in that time, Allen had never washed a dish, changed a diaper, dressed the children, or mowed the lawn. He had come from a background where women were expected to do it all. His mother waited on his dad hand and foot, and of course he was more than happy to continue that lifestyle. Why should he change anything when it had been working for him all these years?

Throughout their marriage, Cynthia had tried everything. She tried being a stay-at-home mom, she worked part time, she held down a full-time job, but no matter what her life was like outside of the home,

Allen's expectations at home remained the same.

She became increasingly nervous while she sat in my chair, and then she began to cry uncontrollably. "I hate him," she said as she sobbed. "Half the time I think I'm losing my mind." She slammed her hand down on the chair, gritted her teeth, and said, "I just can't take it anymore." She became more and more hysterical. "Have you got a copy of the contract you used when you went on strike against Gerald?"

I was completely taken aback. I had been doing Cynthia's hair throughout her marriage, and we knew all about each other's life, so she was fully aware of my strike and how successful it was. But I knew she was not ready to take such a drastic step. If I gave her the contract, she would jump right into it without being prepared. How could I tell her I wasn't going to give her the contract while she was in this hysterical stage?

"I have it at home somewhere," I said while trying to calm her down. "I'll try to find it."

In reality, I knew exactly where the contract was. In fact, I knew exactly where forty-five copies were because I was selling them on the Internet before this book was published.

I calmed Cynthia down by agreeing with her that Allen was a major jerk, but I convinced her that he was a jerk who could be transformed. Just not right now. I finished cutting her hair, sent her on her way to the sweatshop that was her home, and told her I would find the contract and help her come up with a plan.

I went home that night knowing this was not going to be easy. Cynthia was raring to go. I knew it and was determined to slow her down. I knew how long it had taken me to draw up and personally tailor my contract. It took me even longer to be completely certain that I would go through with my own plan. I knew Cynthia hadn't even read the contract.

The biggest reason my domestic strike was a success was because, through the process of drawing up the contract, I slowly realized that my problem wasn't personal. My husband wasn't a jerk, and his disrespect wasn't aimed at me. I saw that the problem wasn't our men. We women were dealing with a societal problem. Somehow I had to make Cynthia understand this before she went forward.

She called me the next day and asked me if I had found the contract. I told her I hadn't found the contract yet, but I did find the guide to make it successful and the list of ten things to do before going ahead with the contract.

I was hoping that if Cynthia was determined to go on strike, she would at least be in possession of the two most important aspects of the endeavor. If I could hold her off long enough and remind her to read these two documents over and over, she would have the battle half won. In the process of studying these two documents she might just experience the epiphany I had gone through. It would let her release the hatred and anger she felt toward her husband. It would let her go through with the strike in a more loving frame of mind and avoid her own emotional blowup.

She came right over. I canceled my lunch break, and we sat down to read through the guide and ten steps together.

"It's very important to get the anger and resentment out of your body before you even start preparing for your strike," I said with tremendous conviction.

"How in the world do you do that?" she asked. Tears transformed her beautifully made-up face into a splotchy mess.

I gently put my hands on her shoulders to be sure to get her attention. "What you do," I said softly and slowly, "is replace your anger and resentment with determination and conviction because once you start, there can be no turning back. First you have to realize that he doesn't do this to you on purpose. He just doesn't know any other way to be."

Cynthia began to settle down a little, and I continued. "Look at his mom. How is he to know he should contribute? The women in his family have always done everything."

"There is no way he could love me and still put me through what he does," Cynthia said. Her anger was rising again, and that terrible thought so many women have was running through her head: he should know what I need without me having to tell him.

"They all do it because we let them," I said. I was adamant. "Allen has no idea how difficult it is to take care of a house and children because he has never done it. Once he experiences it, he will have a whole new respect for you."

"Do you really think so?" Cynthia seemed to have hope for a fleeting moment.

"Only if you have patience and do it right," I said. I put my arms around her. "Now go home and practically memorize the guide and ten steps." I closed her hands around the papers I had given her and sent her on her way.

Two days later, Cynthia called me again. "Have you found the contract yet?" she asked. She seemed urgent, a little too urgent.

"Not yet," I said, "I'm still looking." I somehow knew she was still going to rush it no matter how much I protested.

After a few more phone calls I told her I would call her when I found it.

She made a hair appointment after a couple of weeks, and knowing she was determined to go ahead with things, I took the contract to the salon. However, I also booked her a long appointment so we could plan, which we did.

After about three hours of going over the contract and planning her strategy, I pleaded with Cynthia. "No matter what you do, don't let his anger get to you." I was so afraid she would give in because he knew how his anger had worked in the past. I knew beyond a doubt this leopard's spots wouldn't change. "You have to let him know in no uncertain terms that you can handle his anger because you know this is going to save your marriage and he is worth it," I said. "Let him know you don't blame him for being angry, but you think too much of your marriage to give in. Don't argue, don't explain further—it's all in the contract. When he starts to throw a tantrum, just walk away."

She was gone, and I was a nervous wreck. I knew Allen wouldn't hurt her. He wasn't a violent man, but he did have a short temper.

I couldn't think of much else as I waited for Cynthia to call me and tell me how everything was going. I didn't call her house for fear Allen might be home. I had to remind myself that if Cynthia needed moral support, she would call me.

After about four days, she called me. "It worked," she gushed. "I did what you said, and guess who's fixing dinner tonight."

She was really proud of herself because she had stuck to her guns and let the house go in disarray the whole time. She didn't do anything. Allen had picked up dinner for him and the girls. He didn't do much around the house—it was a mess. But he thought he did a tremendous amount, to the point that he felt exhausted.

The ultimate result was that he did get a brief window into most of the stuff Cynthia was doing and was extremely sorry that he'd overlooked her need for help over the years.

## NOT EVEN CLOSE

Cynthia didn't even come close to getting the results I had achieved because she failed the first hurdle. She caved in before everything was negotiated just because everything seemed to be going wonderfully for the moment. She had seen a little change and assumed more would follow. I can't stress enough how important it is to take full advantage when he finally "gets it."

Cynthia was so excited that—after a few temper tantrums—Allen had become mellow and helpful. She forgot to have him read the whole contract. She forgot to have the whole family decide what ongoing responsibilities belonged to whom. She had essentially quit striking without negotiating long-term changes.

I reminded Cynthia that to get the complete benefit of the strike, she would have had to stay on strike until negotiations were made and chores were spoken for. Now she would have to act again.

I told Cynthia if she didn't continue while the iron was hot, she would only have a temporary solution to a problem that needed a life-time solution. I told her she could and should keep it up. It would be more difficult now because her window of opportunity had closed, but she still had his ear, to a certain extent. She must take full advantage of that, no matter how difficult. Short-term discomfort would be worth a lifetime of change.

Cynthia sat the family down and read the whole contract to all of them. She presented the chore list and had each family member pick out tasks they could be comfortable with forever. Allen balked, but after Cynthia reminded him how much she did in the household and how badly he felt about it just a short time ago, he grudgingly picked out some of the tasks.

Cynthia ended up having a few good days, and Allen at least understood how unfair the whole situation was, but old habits die hard. It wasn't long before Allen was back to his king-of-the-castle ways again.

I can't stress enough not to cave in at the first signs of that four-letter word "help." The real goals of a strike are shared responsibilities and shared respect. That only comes when the husband truly has walked a mile in your shoes.

## IMPROVING THE NEXT GENERATION

Our children will learn about householder responsibilities by our example. What did the children of Cynthia and Allen learn from their parents' example? Very little that will help them in their future relationships because Cynthia eventually let all the family off the hook and most of the householder chores fell back on Mom's weary shoulders. Children should be taught to divide chores with their prospective mate before they marry. Children need to be taught this specifically because the attitude of women has already changed. Young women right now don't want to do it all. Some women want to work outside the home. Some women want to be full-time mothers and homemakers but not family slaves. If boys who are growing up to be future husbands are not ready for this reality, they too will suffer, and their marriages will be explosions waiting to happen.

## REMINDERS

- Don't rush into a strike. To be successful takes planning.
- Focus on love, not resentment.
- Follow through with your strike past his anger, past his first signs of "help," to real negotiation. His empathy will fade, so he must divide chores while his empathy for you is strong.
- Include children in chore selection.
- Children learn by example.

# 19

# WHEN DIVORCE IS NECESSARY

## AND HOW TO PROTECT YOURSELF

> If you have to leave to save your life, once you exit safely, enlist a village to help you.

**I**F YOU ARE IN an abusive relationship, divorce is not only a good idea, but it also may save your life. Please do not suffer in silence. Contact the women's shelter in your area for advice on how to develop your own careful and detailed exit plan. In a way, you will need to prepare thoroughly and in secret in much the same way as I've described planning for a strike. You need to be mentally able to follow your plan completely and not turn back. Above all, realize that you deserve a better life.

In more than forty years as the sounding board for my salon clients, hearing every deep, dark secret about their lives, the one thing my clients never told me about directly was being physically abused by a husband. I learned after the fact, from other people. Why would the subject of spousal abuse be off-limits when every other aspect of a client's life is on the table?

Take Daisy, for example, a client of mine who seemed to be completely in love with her handsome husband, Walter. I had been doing their hair for the fifteen years they had been married. Their two children, Amy and Jennifer, were my clients too. Throughout Daisy and Walter's marriage, I heard the all-too-familiar ups and downs of their lives, but their problems were the kind most couples experience. They had both used me as a sounding board when they had problems, and I thought I knew all about them. To me, they were happy people, and their marriage was super solid.

One day when Daisy sat in my chair, she said, "I always thought I would be married forever. I don't have that forever feeling anymore."

"Well, what has changed?" I asked, shocked at the abrupt change in this seemingly happy union.

"He's been drinking and staying out all night," Daisy said. Then, trying to explain it away, she said, "So 10 percent of my life is awful, but 90 percent of the time, Walter's the most amazing husband in the world."

"If that's the case, then why don't you go to counseling?" I asked.

Daisy agreed, and by the following Friday they had an appointment.

Three days later, Daisy called me and said that Walter had moved out. To say I was floored would be an understatement. It turned out that Walter had planned on leaving all along.

Daisy explained, "He knows that deep down he's probably an alcoholic and he has no plans to stop drinking. He knew that if he stayed with me, he'd have to stop." Then Daisy added, "He also told me he has this twenty-one-year-old girl he'd like to pursue."

That was all she said about it. It was terrible, but I was about to find out a lot more.

I heard through the grapevine that Walter had been putting Daisy down since the early years of their marriage. He had been critical of her housekeeping and even of her mothering. He had constantly reminded her that he thought he was more attractive than she was and that she didn't even deserve him. After Daisy filed for divorce, Walter cleaned up his act for a while. He promised to go to Alcoholics Anonymous. He promised to go to counseling. He told her he would do anything to get her back.

I thought that maybe they would work it out, until one day when Daisy came in for a cut and color. Daisy sat in my chair while her daughter Amy waited. Daisy was saying that she had a restraining order against Walter. In explanation, she told me about a time in their marriage when he had become violent.

I was about to dismiss this accusation as the squabble between a divorcing couple when Amy piped up and said, "Remember when Daddy threw you down the stairs?" Then she looked at me and said, "My mom made me promise I wouldn't call Grandma and Grandpa."

I twirled Daisy around in the chair and blurted out, "I have known you for fifteen years, and you have never even given me a hint about this."

"I never told anyone," Daisy said with tears in her eyes.

## NO ONE DESERVES ABUSE

"When did it start?" I asked. I knew I had to keep the confessions coming because Daisy was very guarded.

"We were out with our friends. He'd been drinking, and our friends had to pull him off me," Daisy said. "One of them told Walter that if he ever hit me again he would kill him. Back then, he didn't punch me, he was just pushing me. He shoved me to the ground."

"What made you think that hurting you was okay?" I asked.

"The first time Walter punched me, we were out with the kids and we were having an argument. He punched me so hard my head hit the window of the car." Daisy was very matter-of-fact while she spoke. "After he hit me, he and the kids went into the restaurant and left me in the car. They didn't even bring me anything to eat. But when they came back, they were chatting away as if nothing had happened. The kids didn't seem to care, so I thought I must have asked for it."

Over the years, I heard women state this reason again and again. They thought they deserved the abuse. It must be one of the reasons nobody had ever confessed domestic violence to me when it happened.

"He didn't do it very often, and it was always after he'd had something to drink," Daisy said. Alcohol was her excuse for Walter's behavior. "After he would hit me, I would actually have the happiest time in my whole marriage. He was always so sorry, and he did everything he could to make it up to me. But after he started drinking so much, his abuse was more frequent, and we all had to walk on eggshells when he was around."

## DIVORCE IN ABUSE CASES IS A BLESSING

Before Daisy told me this story, I was actually hoping that she and her husband could get back together. After her confession, however, I knew she had to be strong and allow the divorce to go through. Walter's promises of going to AA or counseling were only that—promises. He never made any real attempt to follow through, and his demeanor got worse and worse.

Divorce was the only thing Daisy could do to protect herself and her children. She didn't owe Walter her lifetime commitment anymore because Walter didn't honor Daisy's very life. She had to honor her own life. She had to get herself and her girls out.

This is a situation where the option of divorce is a blessing.

Many people, however, use divorce in less severe circumstances. When I urge a couple to work on their marriage, I'm not suggesting that a wife should stay at the risk of her life. Under nonabusive situations, however, ask yourself in all honesty if divorce is really your only option.

## THE LEGAL SYSTEM WILL NOT BE YOUR FRIEND

If divorce is your only option, do it right. The legal system will not be your friend, and you will have to outsmart it every step of the way.

Lawyers on both sides pull out all stops for their own clients. I know this seems like the way it should be, but the important fact getting lost here is that the children should have their own lawyer. I have seen so many situations where the Guardian Ad Litem (advocate for the children) has been bamboozled by the most powerful attorney, and the children's interests get lost in a divorce fight that becomes a war.

## "NO FAULT" IS A TRAVESTY

In my opinion, making divorce "no fault" is one of the biggest mistakes the legal system has made. It means that the innocent people suffer. In the past, the party at fault had to pay more if the other spouse could prove the divorce was his or her fault. If one person wanted out and the other didn't, the one who wanted out had to pay.

If one member of a couple cheats on the other or beats and abuses the other, that party is at fault. He should have to pay more money for what he or she has done. But in a no-fault divorce, even the party who has done wrong can get equal money and equal custody of the kids. The person with the most expensive lawyer gets the most control over the children. And not just in court. I've seen it time and time again where one parent uses money to influence the children against their other parent.

## CONSEQUENCES

Here's an example of the severe consequences of a no-fault divorce:

Sylvia was a beautiful middle-aged woman—blonde hair, blue eyes, and a shape to die for. Her husband, Jim, was a strapping, super-fit man seven years her junior. They had been married for twelve years and seemed to have an ideal relationship. As time went on, though, I noticed a wart here and there. Sylvia did all the work in the office of their thriving business while Jim was constantly flying out of town. They had another business that required someone to be on-call all through the night, and that "someone" always turned out to be her.

Then Sylvia discovered that Jim had a girlfriend.

Sylvia confronted him, and he denied the affair over and over again, even as the proof became more clear.

At times, Sylvia believed Jim when he insisted she must be losing her mind. Her self-esteem plummeted. She finally hired a private detective so she could know if Jim was cheating on her, once and for all.

It turned out that not only did Jim have a girlfriend, but that those frequent flier miles on his credit card were earned on flights to other towns to visit other women. So not only was the cad cheating on Sylvia, he was also cheating on that girl with three other unsuspecting women in different towns.

A divorce was inevitable. The only thing in doubt was the timing.

Sylvia needed positive proof to be used in court, so she kept the private detective on the job and discovered that Jim had conducted himself in the same manner—cheating with multiple women—in his previous marriage. After a significant amount of time and reams of evidence, Sylvia filed for divorce.

The divorce court, however, turned out to be a nightmare. The law had just changed to make divorce "no fault." So all of the evidence she had gathered so meticulously was for naught. Sylvia did receive a good settlement in the divorce decree. She got portions of the property and holdings because she had indisputably worked so hard to make the businesses successful. Jim, however, got the businesses themselves, and the holdings Sylvia received in the divorce decree were to be given to her monthly by him.

That lasted only a little while, and then Jim miraculously began losing large amounts of money in a business that had previously been prospering.

Sylvia's payments dried up.

She called her lawyer, took Jim back to court, and he was ordered to pay. He would pay a few times and then stop again. Because they didn't have children, Sylvia couldn't even call child protective services to get Jim to make his payments.

Months went by. Every time Sylvia hired an attorney and went to court, the court costs and attorney fees ate up all of what she had won in court. The stress of worrying about her finances from month to month took a heavy toll on her health. She gave up and got a job in a department store and has been living sparsely ever since.

## PROTECT YOURSELF

As a divorcing woman, you have to protect yourself. Your lawyer isn't in this to take care of you. He or she is in it for the money.

Take the following example:

Julia's daughter, Heather, was going through a divorce. Her husband was leaving her for another woman. I was so happy Julia was supportive of her only daughter, spending long hours on the phone and even hopping on an airplane when things got really tough.

Every time Julia came into the salon, I reminded her to put a certain stipulation in the divorce settlement. She would have just arrived home from a visit to Heather, and pushy me would nag: "Did you tell Heather to put the stipulation in the final judgment?"

"I forgot," she'd say, over and over.

Finally, after being told "I forgot" and "She'll tell her attorney," a number of times, I got a definitive answer. The stipulation had been added.

Fast-forward to eight months after the divorce, when the ex-husband had moved across the country. The infamous scenario did come up. He was three months behind on his child support. But, thanks to the stipulation, he had to travel all the way from L.A. to New York—where Heather lived—and pay all of Heather's costs just to go back to court. It didn't take him any time at all to figure out it was much less expensive to pay his child support on time.

Imagine if Heather had been the one who was responsible for all that money and inconvenience, as many women are.

Heather's attorney told her, "That was an ingenious idea of yours." But, really, you can't tell me that among all the brilliant attorneys, no one has thought of this.

## MONEY-SAVING DECREE STIPULATION

The stipulation that Heather included in her final judgment read like this: "If for any reason a husband does not follow through with orders to pay child support or alimony as already stipulated in the divorce decree, any attorney fees and out-of-pocket expenses incurred in the process of enforcing the order must be the husband's responsibility."

This clause doesn't cover a trip back to court to increase child support or to change anything that's already been settled. All this clause does is protect the original decree. It also protects the children.

Your attorney is there to make a living. It isn't to his or her benefit to have this stipulated in the divorce papers because every time you go to court, lawyers make money. Lawyers would probably be happy to see you in court once a week.

These sound like horror stories because they are. I want you to see the real suffering people go through to get divorced. It's painful. It's expensive. Very often, women don't even end up with the money that is their legal due. Their standard of living decreases by almost half after a divorce, and those whose husbands get out of their payments altogether end up even worse.

## AFTER DIVORCE

Few lives are made better by a divorce. Women who are suffering abuse and neglect have to take the leap, but not all of the 17 million divorced adults in America look back thinking that their divorce was worth the emotional and financial losses they suffered to get it.

One of my clients, Andrea, suffered tremendously to get her divorce, and her husband was an unscrupulous man she probably never should have married. One day, when she was at my salon, she opened up a bill her ex-husband was supposed to have paid. He hadn't paid it, nor had he been paying the alimony or child support payments. Her eight-dollar-an-hour job didn't even come close to paying the bills.

"I've got to call my lawyer," she said, sobbing. "He can't get away with this."

She called the lawyer from my salon. When she got off the phone, her face was white as a sheet. She wasn't crying. I can only explain her demeanor as that of someone who had lost all hope for anything and was giving up.

"The lawyer said he can't do another thing for me until I pay my bill with him," she said.

I knew she couldn't. Her ex-husband's lawyer had been paid because her ex-husband still had the business that Andrea too had worked hard to make a success.

I thought she might go to social services so they could confiscate his wages. We were in for another surprise there.

The ex-husband suddenly had no wages. He had been liquidating all of his holdings among friends and family so he could avoid paying Andrea and the children their due. Even worse, he was setting himself up so his ultimate plan could come to fruition: To file for *bankruptcy*.

This was probably the worst case I saw in a divorce.

This was a family who had been extremely prosperous. They had a super-upscale home with a swimming pool and all the amenities. After the divorce, they were each living in rented mobile homes. However, the husband's poverty was intentional and short-lived. In a few years, he got his business back on track. Andrea remained in poverty.

This was a marriage that screamed for divorce. Andrea's husband had no redeeming qualities. He had completely failed my "Rule of the Ruler" test.

## SURPRISING CONSEQUENCE

Ironically, when I told Andrea I was writing this book, she said, "Make sure you let everyone know the consequences of a divorce."

She surprised me completely by what she said next.

"If I had it to do over again, I would have stayed."

"Even with his habitual girl chasing?" I asked. "Even with his lies?"

"Yes, even with that," Andrea said. "And do you know why? Because when we were married, the kids got along. After I left him— right from the get-go—even though they had all begged me to divorce their dad, the kids immediately took his side. And do you know the reason? Not only did he have a silver tongue, but he was also the one with the money."

I was beginning to understand.

"It's been twenty years since the divorce, and not one time have the children all been in unison," Andrea said. "They have absolutely hated each other at times. Because of the divorce, they've felt as though they had to take sides. A family reunion is definitely out of the question."

Andrea looked at me through the mirror.

"I wouldn't want to have stayed for him, but only so I could have my family."

Isn't it sad? I can't even imagine a scenario where staying would have been good for Andrea. However, the situation she ultimately found herself in wasn't good either.

And second marriages are rarely any better than the first ones. People tend to have the same problems they had before but also have to deal with resentment from kids and stepkids.

So be careful. Think twice. Life after divorce is harder than you imagine.

## REMINDERS

- Do not stay in a marriage in which you are being hurt and abused. Leave carefully and with a detailed exit plan. Seek advice from your local women's shelter on how to leave safely.
- Absolutely no one deserves to be hurt and abused by her spouse.
- If, because of abuse or other irreconcilable difference, divorce is your only option, remember that the legal system will not be your friend.
- Advocate for yourself and your children.
- Include the stipulation in your child support or alimony decree that the defaulting party pay travel and court costs.
- Be fully aware of the consequences of divorce before you enter this tunnel of horrors.

# 20

# EVERYTHING I KNOW ABOUT CHORES I LEARNED FROM MY MOTHER

> Children love structure. They need structure. It prevents chaos and adds to their confidence and self-esteem.

**L** OUIS ANSPACHER WROTE, "Marriage is a relationship . . . in which the independence is equal, the dependence mutual, and the obligation reciprocal." We can teach our children that the woman of the household is *not* responsible for all of the work in the household. We can teach our children to do chores. Even better, we can teach them *how* to do chores properly and promptly so they can be true helpmates in their coming marriages. I sincerely hope that eventually, household sharing will be incorporated into the high school curriculum and that premarriage counseling will include divvying up the chores and responsibilities.

As the one person who knows what it takes to run a smoothly functioning house (because you've been doing all those chores yourself), you have an extra responsibility to fulfill. You can't delegate this one. When you and your family divide up the chores (whether after a mini- or full strike or without one), don't forget that you'll probably have to teach your children (and maybe your husband) how to do the chores on their lists.

Don't patronize. Don't expect everyone to do things your way just for the sake of maintaining control. But also don't expect a ten-year-old who has never lifted a finger to know how to run the washer and dryer without some training first. Take time to show the children the right way to do it and perhaps post a card with the steps. You'll avoid the frustration and poor self-esteem that come with doing a job poorly. You don't want to nag. If they give up, too often we take back the chore as our own, defeating ourselves and spoiling our children. Engage your children in cleaning right now so they can be equal helpmates to their spouses in the future.

## "I THOUGHT SHE WAS WATCHING ME!"

One woman told me, "I don't know why my daughter is such a poor housekeeper. I kept my house spotless. She was there. I thought she was watching me." Don't count on it! But there is one thing kids quickly pick up by being in the presence of a mom who does it all: they learn that they don't have to do any work around the house, that they can make and leave messes because someone else will clean up after them.

When dividing responsibilities, make sure that your male children take on some of the indoor chores and your female children take on some of the outdoor chores. De-emphasize the notion that there are male and female chores. Stress to the children the reason they must learn to be responsible for householder chores: so they can gain the skills to have balanced marriages and happy lives.

Imagine each habit making a pathway through their brains. The more a performance is repeated, the clearer that habit pathway becomes. Think about it. If you have a commitment that requires getting up at five o'clock every morning for a year, it becomes almost impossible for you to sleep past five o'clock. The goal here is to form good habit trails in children as they grow. If your children have already done a good deal of their growing, then your goal is to help them form good habit trails now for the future. Nobody is ever too old to learn.

## CHORES CAN TURN BOYS INTO MEN

It's wonderful to begin training your children when they're young, but if you're already past that stage, don't despair. You can adapt these chores and teaching methods to older children too. Just show and tell them how to do each chore as you do it together. Don't use a patronizing voice, of course, but don't assume that your child understands the steps involved in any chore without having been expressly taught them first.

Nothing in this chapter is partial to one gender. It is just as crucial to teach boys good housekeeping habits and rules as it is girls. In fact, one responsible young man I know was asked what made him so efficient in his construction job. Although his job included some of the most hefty, masculine labor one could perform, the young man said, "I learned everything I know from doing household chores as a kid."

## THE TWO KINDS OF CHORES

There is an easy way to approach chores to get results. Consider first the two types of chores:

- Immediate Chores
- Daily, Weekly, and Periodic Chores

## IMMEDIATE CHORES (THOSE EVERYDAY MESSES)

Immediate chores are not listed in the Fair Marriage Contract, but you will make your life much easier if you teach your children (and husband) to do them right now, regardless of whether you're planning a strike.

Immediate chores are messes brought on by situations, and they happen a hundred times each day. If you take off your coat, you've got an immediate chore on your hands: you've got to put your coat away (instead of dropping it in the hallway). If you spill a glass of juice, you've got an immediate chore of cleaning up the spill. If you take your keys out of the ignition, you've got an immediate chore of putting the keys where you can find them next time. Very often, we leave the clothes on the bed and the spills on the floor. We leave the keys in a pocket, but we can't remember which one.

We don't always respond to the immediate chore. We either save it for later or ignore it entirely. The problem with this approach is that while immediate chores are tiny, they stack up. Soon, every surface in the house is covered with something, the keys are lost, and someone is hollering. The only person the whole family (including you) looks at to be responsible is Mom.

## BE AN EXAMPLE

(Okay, our secret!) You might have to train yourself to do immediate chores while you train your children and husband to do them. Notice when you think it's okay to leave your shoes by the front door when you come in and how they seem part of a larger mess later. Notice whether you fully clean the kitchen after a meal or whether you leave the drips of food on the stove to harden another night. Notice how these habits make more work for you later in the day or week. Begin doing your immediate chores as soon as they arise.

## THE MINUTE MEN (AND WOMEN)

One way to teach your children to do immediate chores is to remind them to be minute people. You have to demonstrate this behavior yourself and state it as you do a chore.

- The minute we get up, we make our beds.
- The minute we bring books and papers home from school, we put them in the designated study area.
- The minute we take off our socks, we fold them together and put them in the hamper.
- The minute we take off our pajamas, we put them away.
- The minute we get through with any tool, we put it back in its proper place.

My father used to tell me something when he held up his pocketknife. "See this?" he'd ask. "I've had this knife for twenty years. It has *never* in all that time been anywhere but in my pocket or in my hand. When I change clothes, the first thing I do is place my pocketknife in the pocket of my clean pair of pants."

## TEACHING TODDLERS

Healthy children come equipped with a boundless amount of ambition. If you don't harness that energy and channel it into constructive areas, it's likely that they will use it for destruction. You're familiar with the terrible twos: children that age can dump a whole sack of flour on the floor, paint the white tiles with red nail polish, and pour molasses through the toaster before you can blink twice.

But you have one thing going for you at this age: They love to be around Mommy or Daddy. Make the most of this asset. While Mommy is cleaning the kitchen, give the toddler a damp dishcloth and let him wash off the chairs and appliances. Let him help make the beds, dust the furniture, and sort the clothes. You won't get a lot of help at this point—in fact, the child will make more messes as he tries to help—but there are bonuses:

1. It's an excellent opportunity to form good habits.
2. It keeps them so busy and happy, they won't be tearing the house apart further.
3. They'll learn that doing chores is a great way to interact with you.

A lady I know was sorting socks one day while watching her two grandchildren, Landon, three, and Krystal, eighteen months. While Grandma was busy piling up the socks by color, the two toddlers were busy throwing the socks from the sorted piles back into any old pile they happened to land in. It was okay with Grandma because the children were having the time of their lives and so was Grandma—and they were doing something together.

## EXPLAIN WHAT YOU'RE DOING AND WHY

As you take the time to teach your children, they learn that everything has its proper place and that they should put things back in their places when finished. That is, *if* you take the time to teach them. You have to tell children what you are doing and why you are doing it at every turn. Don't think they will pick it up through osmosis by growing up in your do-it-all presence. You have to teach them.

For instance, get your daughter and son their own little broom with its own little nail to hang it on. After you are through sweeping the floor together, tell your child, "We must always put things back when we are through with them." In our family, my husband is responsible for shoveling the snow. Yes, it's a traditionally masculine job, but he taught our sons and daughter to do it too. So he got the children their own little shared snow shovel with its own little nail. Then he worked with one child at a time, explaining the chore while they shoveled together.

His pattern went something like this: "We need to make sure we always shovel the snow off before anyone walks on it so it won't turn to ice. Watch what can happen. Step in that fresh snow. Now shovel it away. See how your snowy footprints stick to the sidewalk? They will turn to ice. We wouldn't want anyone to slip on the ice and get hurt, would we? Okay. Now, where do we put the snow shovel when we're finished with it?"

## RITUALS MAKE IT EASIER

You should establish three important rituals in your home: A time to get up, a time for each meal, and bedtime. I've known small children who were in bed by seven-thirty. Sleeping had become such a habit for them that no one had to wake them up in the mornings. After playing all day, they were ready to go to sleep at bedtime, and after sleeping all night, they were up early, feeling refreshed.

Rituals make life predictable. If cleaning up is part of mealtime every single time, your children (and your husband) will simply know not to go off and play or watch television until the kitchen is cleaned. At our house, we say it this way: The recreation is your dessert. We don't have dessert until we have completed the main course, which includes the cleaning process.

Meals and cleanup afterward are rituals in our house, but snack time isn't. Snack time is separate from mealtime. If children are hungry between meals, teach them to clean up after themselves when they get a snack, or the kitchen will be a constant disaster.

## DAILY, WEEKLY, PERIODIC, AND SPECIAL OCCASION CHORES

Daily, weekly, periodic, and special occasion chores are listed in the Fair Marriage Contract. We need to cook meals, clean up after meals, and perhaps run a few loads of laundry daily. Maybe we vacuum and mop the floors weekly. Periodic chores are those things you do only a few times a year, such as wash the walls and windows, change the furnace filter, and shovel snow (unless you live in Alaska). Special occasion chores are those things you do to get ready for a trip or holiday and those things you do when the trip or holiday is over. These chores include making reservations, packing and unpacking suitcases, stringing holiday lights, buying or making Halloween costumes, and putting away all the holiday decorations.

When you sit down with the Fair Marriage Contract, each family member will choose the daily, periodic, and special occasion chores for which he or she wants to be responsible. You might find that your husband does a great deal of the periodic chores already. He may clean the cars, change the furnace filter, check the plumbing, and do household construction projects. He gets to put his name next to these items, and you get to appreciate him for having done them all these years.

Here are a few examples of how you can train your children to do their daily, periodic, and special occasion chores. Not every chore is described, of course, but you can use the following methods to train your children to do any chore they need to do.

## CLEANING THE KITCHEN

Young children can be taught to do all the chores associated with cleaning the kitchen. Choose all or one of these chores and train your child until the habit trail has been fixed in his mind.

For example, Mommy fills a dish pan full of warm, soapy dish water and then has Johnny clear all the dishes off the table and put them in the pan in the sink. She says, "Okay, you are going to let the dish water work for you and be soaking the dishes while you brush the crumbs off the counters with a dishcloth."

Give him a somewhat sloshy-wet dishcloth and show him how to hold it. Most kids who haven't been taught wad it up into a little ball. This does not work at all. The dishcloth should be flattened out. Teach Johnny to flatten his hand over the cloth and use his thumb and part of his fingers to go over the edges of the counter and up the sides while he is wetting them down. This is another time he can let the water work for him. He wets all the counters down rather rapidly with just enough water that the counter is wet but not dripping.

"Now, Johnny," you say, "you did that really well." I'll show you how to wring out the dishcloth, and you can start over on the first counters you wet down. It's easy to get all the dirt off now because the water has been working for you. Sometimes the counters already look clean, but they are not. There are little germs that we can't see that we need to wipe off every day."

This will become a daily routine for Johnny or Suzie eventually. Teach them each and every step as you go.

Wring the cloth out for him after he wipes each counter and then give him a dry dish towel and help him go over the counters again. "Now," you say, "do you want to see how to check whether it's really clean?" Have him run his bare little hand over each surface. Ask him, "Is it smooth or bumpy? If it's smooth, it's clean. If it's rough, you need to go over it again." He usually doesn't have to at this point because the kitchen was thoroughly cleaned the night before. But it teaches him how to double check.

### Sweeping the Floor

His floor-sweeping skills will get better as he gets big enough to handle a broom, but he will be so happy if you let him do it anyway. Choose a small section of the floor, not the whole thing. Say to him,

"See this row of squares? Pretend this broom is a road grader and this row of squares is the road." Show him how to hold the broom and give him an imaginary line on the floor as a barrier. Tell him, "When you get to this line, go back and do the next road." Demonstrate on the first two rows of squares what you mean. Then let him do the rest. When he gets that done, let him do the next section. Demonstrate as many times as he needs to learn the procedure.

When the dirt is all gathered up in a little pile, you say, "Okay, now it's Mommy's turn. I'm going to see if you missed any spots. Watch me closely and see where I get my dirt."

This is an ongoing process. I've heard a child as old as twelve say to his brother, "I know where Mom gets all her dirt. She gets it on the mop boards, under the stove, in the broom closet, and right here under the door stopping." They love the challenge of trying a little harder each day. Of course, Mommy plays this up by saying, "Wow, you are getting better every day! I hardly got any dirt this time!"

## Washing the Dishes

If you have a dishwasher, let Johnny rinse the dishes and put them in the dishwasher. Then he wipes up the countertop and is finished. Of course, you might have to teach him to wash dishes by hand.

When I was a little girl, washing dishes was my chore. I said to my mother, "Mom, let's buy a dishwasher."

Mom said, "Why in the world would we need a dishwasher? We already have one."

"I know," I said. "That's why we need one."

See, the kitchen was easy. There weren't many dishes. It probably took you longer to read all the tips than it took Johnny to clean it. You say, "Johnny! You cleaned this whole kitchen by yourself! I'm so-o proud of you!" But most of all, Johnny is proud of himself. You say, "Guess what? As soon as you get a little bigger, I'll *let* you mop the floor!" Or she might say something like, "If you can clean up even faster next time and beat the buzzer, I'll *let* you help make some cookies." (Of course, allow plenty of time for him to beat the buzzer when he's young.)

## NOT "YOU HAVE TO" BUT INSTEAD "I'LL LET YOU"

The key phrase here is "I'll let you." Program habits into young minds that make them believe each added task is a privilege. Instead of saying "you have to," you say, "you get to."

Talk to children on their own level. They love to pretend. They love to play with Daddy and Mommy.

I told a four-year-old niece one time when her mother's vacuum was in the repair shop, "Pretend you are a vacuum cleaner, get down on the carpet, pick up all the little pieces of lint and paper, and put them in this bag."

All excited and willing to please, little Spring got down on all fours and said, "Okay, I'm ready. Will you hold my legs up?" She carried that one a little far, but isn't that how kids think?

## IT ONLY TOOK THAT LONG?

Before you ever have your child do a chore, have him or her time the chore as you do it to see how long it really takes. This will help the child understand that a chore doesn't have to take up the entire day, and that a chore done daily (with gusto!) takes only minutes. You can even do this later in the learning process if the child is feeling sluggish or overwhelmed by the task.

Together, note the time on the clock before you get started and note it again once you finish.

"Okay," you'll ask, "how long did that take?"

She'll say, "Not quite five minutes."

"Of course you have five minutes a day to see to it that your chore is done," you say. The task isn't overwhelming now; it's just a little five-minute chore.

Assign chores to yourself in this way too. You won't mind cleaning out one cabinet shelf a day; you will mind emptying everything and scrubbing it all at once, even if you only do it a few times a year.

## THE CHECK-OFF LIST

Post the chore list from the Fair Marriage Contract somewhere the whole family can refer to it. Of course the adults and older children in the family will know what their chores are just by looking at this list. Younger children, however, will require you to make them a specific kind of chore list.

At this stage, they need each little part of each chore outlined for them, like when you first learned to operate a stick shift on a car. At first you had to consciously think about each step, but you soon learned the routine. It formed deeper and deeper habit trails in your mind until the whole process became so much a part of you that you could do it automatically, hardly giving it a second thought.

Look at the following example for a four-year-old whose chore is to clear off the table after dinner. The list assumes that an older child or adult has removed the heavy food platters and knives from the table before the child begins:

| | Mon | Tue | Wed | Thu | Fri | Sat | Sun |
|---|---|---|---|---|---|---|---|
| Carry plates to sink | | | | | | | |
| Carry glasses to sink | | | | | | | |
| Carry silverware to sink | | | | | | | |
| Carry cloth napkins to hamper (paper to trash) | | | | | | | |
| Wipe table with wet dishcloth | | | | | | | |
| Rinse dishcloth in sink | | | | | | | |
| Hang dishcloth to dry | | | | | | | |
| Wash your hands | | | | | | | |

Don't assume that a young child will know what "clear the table" means. Go ahead and outline every single step of the process for her and let her put a check mark by each step once she's done it.

You can put a sticker on her chart once she's completed the chore for the day. This small token will help her feel good about doing her part, whereas older children and adults will feel good about doing their part because they will perceive the new sense of peace and cooperation in the house.

You will find age-appropriate lists in the appendix at the back of this book. You can simply photocopy them and post them on your refrigerator or you can change and adapt them to your family's needs. Be sure you've taught your kids every skill you want them to be able to do before you have them do the chores by themselves. Doing chores one knows how to do well will create feelings of accomplishment and success. But doing chores one doesn't know how to do well will make the child feel overwhelmed, resentful, and afraid of failure.

Don't overwhelm everyone with chores. The purpose of this process is to make the lives of everyone in the family more balanced.

Once you and your children get into the habit of doing your immediate chores immediately and your daily chores daily, you will all see that the chores can be done easily the more often they're done. You'll see that in time, what took you an hour to accomplish now only takes a half hour. Point this out to your children and occasionally bring out the timer and show them how much faster they're getting at their chores.

The children will eventually have the system down pat. They'll know what it takes to do each chore. It's like becoming police officers: you can only prepare to do dangerous work if you practice your moves over and over in a safe environment. When police officers are forced into conflict, their training takes over and the techniques they've practiced come naturally to them. They have to do this because in most cases, they don't have time to stop and think about what to do. Your kids may never be in a life-or-death situation when it comes to mopping the floor, but they should be able to do their chores quickly and easily. That way the chores won't get in the way of their homework, time with friends, or anything else. And most important, chores—or the avoidance of chores—won't get in the way of them having happy marriages when they become adults.

## DON'T FIGHT ABOUT IT!

You've been on strike. Your kids understand how much you used to do, 24/7. They experienced the crisis that erupted when Mom quit doing everything. Now they realize their role as part of the household and householder chores. Nevertheless, your teenage children and even your husband may continue to complain about doing their chores. Don't fall for this. Don't engage in an argument. It's not their job to do the chores happily; it's their job to do the chores. Period. If they want to complain or argue, you can tell them, "Complain or not, that's your job." And leave it at that.

## REMINDERS

- As hard as it is, it's important to teach your children to do chores—for your sake and for their sakes both now and as future adults in balanced households.
- Two kinds of chores exist: immediate (tiny but cumulative messes to be cleaned up by their makers) and daily, weekly, or periodic (chores to be divided among householders).
- Start teaching your children young, when they love to be around Mommy and Daddy and want to please them. But even older kids can take on new habits.
- Make sure boys and girls have indoor and outdoor chores to avoid a gender-bias attitude toward chores.
- Timing how long it takes to do a chore often challenges kids to do better than you (or shows they are improving). It also removes the easy excuse, "I don't have time."

# EPILOGUE

The way we see the problem, is the problem.

**MY ULTIMATE GOAL** in writing this book is to change the thinking in our society. Go back a few steps in one instance and take a giant leap forward in another. In going back a few steps, we must erase the idea that people unhappy in their marriages must get out. Barring any abuse, what ever happened to "until death do us part"?

It may seem ridiculous to quote wedding vows because people make them and break them over and over. It's relatively common to have been divorced twice or more. We need to open our eyes and examine where this flippant thinking is taking us and its toll on families and society. The real-life stories in this book show that the belief in divorce as a quick fix to our troubles is defeating us all. We need to return to the idea of making marriage work no matter what we have to do. We need to believe in keeping our children under the same roof with both parents.

In moving forward a giant leap, we have to change the way we think about householder responsibility. I believe it will be a much greater challenge but well worth the effort. My story proves that it is entirely possible to wake a sleeping giant (my husband!), cause him to be aware of the inequality happening under his nose, right that inequality, and become happy together once again. I traded my own resentment, unhappiness, anger, and ultimate hopelessness for empathy, love, and the realization that my husband was never bad, he had just been misinformed.

It's going to be difficult at best to feed and nurture this idea. After all, we collectively believe that women are responsible for doing it all, a thought that has been deeply embedded in our society and our psyches. Many women are angry and in despair because they feel doing it all is their lot in life and nothing can change the overwhelming burden. Men, for their part, often feel we're putting them down when we stand up for ourselves.

As you read this book, you may have realized that going on strike and using the other techniques I discuss are not at all unfair to men. They form a reasonable plan to turn Mr. Clueless into an equal partner to make your marriage happier and more stable. When two people in the household are working full time and only one of them is responsible for the second job, which is the household, resentment flourishes and causes so much anger that, in too many cases, the quick-fix answer is divorce. My fervent desire is to do something to remove that cause for anger—the imbalance of householder chores—and thereby stop the divorce rate from skyrocketing. Our children will thank us both as children and as adults.

By reading this book, you are showing that you're ready to help those you love become responsible for their share of the householder work. You're ready to trade in resentment for change. You're ready to let your husband and children take on their share of the work. And you're ready to train your children to do the work properly.

Just remember, we can spend our time doing every chore and being responsible for everything around the house, creating resentment and anger. Or we can share everything: our chores, our love for each other, and our time with our children. Most important, we can have time for relationships that are free from resentment, anger, and hopelessness and full of love and happiness.

Now, if you have done all you need to do and are ready to go on strike, copy the Fair Marriage Contract and appendix B (which is the list of chores). Also copy chapter 17, "Thoughts to Keep You Strong and Sustain Your Love."

If you and your partner have mutually agreed to divide the chores without a strike, print up the chore list itself—appendix B.

Photocopy everything you need and make changes according to your lifestyle and needs. Best wishes for a happy, balanced future!

# APPENDIX A
# THE FAIR MARRIAGE CONTRACT

PROPOSED CONTRACT

## The Fair Marriage Contract

TO BE NEGOTIATED
BY BOTH PARTIES

## THE FAIR MARRIAGE CONTRACT

It is the intention of this contract to effectively guide balanced and efficient operations of a household and at the same time provide against the workload abuse and unfair treatment of female householders.

The major purpose for negotiations between male and female householders is to set forth expectations and obligations so as to promote peaceful and loving relationships between parties at all levels. The goal is a sustained effort by all parties to achieve a loving home and smooth-running operations. The balancing of chores aims to eliminate nonperformance caused by overload of female householder duties, resulting in occupational illness, extreme fatigue, and/or resentment.

Eliminating unfair and unhealthy working conditions would automatically remove overburden and occupational health hazards and yield a stability to household operations, reduce emotional problems for all householders, improve communications between adult householders, and increase mutual respect.

## HIGHLIGHTS OF PROPOSED EXPECTATIONS

| | |
|---|---|
| I | Classifications and Responsibilities |
| II | Coverage of Compensation |
| III | Preservation of Health and Safety Rights |
| IV | Personal and Sick Leave |
| V | Holidays and Vacations |
| VI | Discrimination |
| VII | Settlement of Disputes |
| VIII | Addendum—Chore Lists |

# I

## CLASSIFICATIONS

1.  Female householder at home full time.
2.  Female householder working outside the home full time.

## RESPONSIBILITIES
### to be done or delegated by

1.  Female householder at home full time:

    a.  Housekeeping
    b.  Shopping
    c.  Cooking
    d.  Laundry
    e.  Nursing
    f.  Chauffeuring
    g.  Social Secretary
    h.  Managing Children's Affairs
    i.  Record Keeping

(NOTE: These and other chores to be shared with all household members on weekends and after school or after male householder's job as negotiated in this contract—VIII Addendum.)

2.  Female householder working outside the home full time:

SHARE ALL RESPONSIBILITIES with all household members as negotiated in this contract—VIII Addendum.

## II

## COVERAGE OF COMPENSATION

1. COMPENSATIONS FOR FEMALE HOUSEHOLDER AT HOME FULL TIME:

   a. Weekly allowance for personal use.
   b. Integrate housework among all householders, taking male householder's full-time job restrictions into consideration.

2. COMPENSATIONS FOR FEMALE HOUSEHOLDER WORKING OUTSIDE THE HOME FULL TIME:

   a. If householder duties are shared 50/50, the employed female householder shares her income with the household and is a full partner in all financial and domestic projects.
   b. If all householder duties are done or delegated by employed female householder, a significant portion of money coming from the female householder's full-time job shall be earmarked for hiring out some or all of the housekeeping duties, as the female householder sees necessary for creating balance and leisure in her own life.

## III

## PRESERVATION OF HEALTH AND SAFETY RIGHTS

1. Female householder will alternate obligations of being on call 24 hours a day, 365 days a year with male householder.

2. Alternating on-call obligations will result in female householder's freedom to make decisions without first making arrangements for the kids and household to be taken care of, as the entire burden will no longer rest on her shoulders.

## IV

## PERSONAL AND SICK LEAVE

1. When female householder is ill, all her duties will be taken over completely by other householders until female householder recuperates.

    a. All duties will be performed so female householder does not have double-duty when she recuperates.


## V

## HOLIDAYS AND VACATIONS

1. All holidays should be for the enjoyment of all householders with preparations and cleanup shared by all householders.

2. Any work required in preparation for, during, or returning from vacations should be shared mutually by all householders.


## VI

## DISCRIMINATION

1. No person shall be discriminated against.

    a. No person shall be discriminated against on basis of wages earned.
    b. No person shall be coerced into a job unsuitable for his or her skills or time constraints.
    c. No person shall be put down. Put-downs such as "You're just a housewife" or "What do you do all day?" from either party shall result in said complainer doing the at-home duties of the other party for a full weekend.

# VII

## SETTLEMENT OF DISPUTES

1.  Male and female householder may choose the means best suited for them in settling disputes, whether orally or in writing.

    a.  Oral dispute settlement will be used to express oneself verbally ONLY if one is best suited to do so and only if one is calm enough to discuss the matter without violence or put-downs.
    b.  Written dispute settlement will be used to express oneself if one is verbally intimidated or if one is best suited to express oneself on paper.

2.  VERBAL ABUSE BY EITHER PARTY IS NOT ACCEPTABLE.

_____        _____
Signature of Female Householder          Date


_____        _____
Signature of Male Householder            Date


_____        
Notary Signature                         Notary Seal

If contract is broken, this gives the female householder authority to go on strike and remain on strike until such time that male householder can go over grievances and negotiate disputes. Fair practices to all household members must result so an agreement can be ratified.

This is not a legal contract and must be taken to the appropriate parties to be legalized. The author of this contract is not liable for any outcome that may result in the signing of said contract.

## VIII

## ADDENDUM TO THE CONTRACT

The List of Householder Chores to be divided fairly among all householders.

1. Chore division will be spread fairly among all parties while taking time constraints into consideration.

2. Chores assigned will be taken on as the full responsibility of the signing householder for life or until a time of further negotiation.

# APPENDIX B
## HOUSEHOLDER CHORE LISTS

**I**N THIS SECTION you will find day-by-day, week-by-week, and month-by-month lists of responsibilities to be shared. Sit your entire family down together and have everyone choose the chores he or she will take on permanently. Be sure you train your children to do the chores they pick and be sure you don't allow a child to pick a chore that's too difficult or one that's inappropriate.

If you're going on strike, photocopy the chore lists and put them with your strike contract after page 7 of the Fair Marriage Contract—Addendum to the Contract. Your chore list is the addendum.

If you are not going on strike but you feel you can negotiate a realignment of householder duties with your fellow householders, photocopy just the chore lists.

### RESPONSIBILITY FOR SELF

If you'd like every member of your household to take on a certain chore for himself or herself (packing for vacations, for example), just write "Individual" next to that chore.

### FINANCIAL CHORES

In many cases, these jobs go together in one lump or you risk your finances becoming haphazard. You can also take these chores on together; figure out who is the more responsible when it comes to paying bills on time; or determine who is more skilled at investments, insurance, and other money matters.

It's essential that both partners know what is going on with their money, however, so if you don't take on the money chore together, be sure to update your partner on the state of your finances and savings every few months.

Taking on financial chores counts as seven chores in our household: sorting and answering mail, paying bills, making deposits, arranging for financial gifts, paying children's school dues, managing investments, and updating partner on money matters. Break down all the parts of money matters as they occur in your life and count each part as one chore.

## CHORES FOR CAMPING (OR OTHER RECREATION)

My family loves to go camping. The chores for camping are so different than the chores one might have on another kind of trip that we had to have a separate chore list for it. I include it for you to photocopy if you need it. Be sure to leave it out if your family doesn't camp or modify it to fit the type of recreation your family pursues.

Does your family like to snowshoe on Sundays? Are you do-it-yourselfers who love to spend a weekend building a closet or porch? Use the camping list as a guide and list the necessary chores for any activity your family does regularly. Then divide those up. You'll find a blank chart for doing this at the end of the camping chore list.

## CHORES FOR YOUNG CHILDREN

To make young children feel included—and to let them know that living in a house is everyone's responsibility—let even your youngest children pick an appropriate chore from the list. Daily chores for young children are listed separately. These chores are actually the things you and the child have to do together every day: eat breakfast, put the bowl in the sink or dishwasher, brush teeth, and so on. If you turn these daily habits into little chores, your child will learn to do chores from the start. You can take this time to train the child to clean up after herself in all she does. She not only brushes her teeth (or has them brushed for her), she puts her toothbrush back in its holder and wipes the edge of the sink. I have known people to use this list with babies, telling them everything they are doing as Mommy does it. As soon as the child begins to toddle, she has heard that you put pajamas in the hamper a hundred times, and she's fully prepared to do it herself.

## PERIODIC CHORES

As you write the name of the householder who'll be taking on each periodic chore, you'll need to decide when some of these chores must be done. You can write the date the chore must be completed or you can write a deadline the chore must be completed by. (Example: The ovens will be cleaned by January 15, April 15, July 15, and November 15 each year or they must be cleaned on January 15, April 15, July 15, and November 15.) If you list specific dates, be sure to leave leeway in case of emergencies, changes of plans, and special events.

## A LAST NOTE

Photocopy everything you need and make changes according to your lifestyle.

## CHORE LIST FOR TODDLERS AND YOUNG CHILDREN

This entire list is intended for one child to use every day. You can help the child put a check mark or small sticker next to each chore every day.

### CHORES FOR TODDLERS AND YOUNG CHILDREN

| | Mon | Tue | Wed | Thu | Fri | Sat | Sun |
|---|---|---|---|---|---|---|---|
| Wake up politely | | | | | | | |
| Eat breakfast | | | | | | | |
| Put dish in sink or dishwasher | | | | | | | |
| Brush teeth | | | | | | | |
| Put toothbrush away | | | | | | | |
| Dry edge of sink | | | | | | | |
| Choose clothes | | | | | | | |
| Get dressed | | | | | | | |
| Put pajamas in drawer or hamper | | | | | | | |
| Make bed | | | | | | | |
| Eat lunch | | | | | | | |
| Put dish in sink or dishwasher | | | | | | | |
| Eat dinner | | | | | | | |
| Put dish in sink or dishwasher | | | | | | | |
| Take bath | | | | | | | |
| Empty bathtub | | | | | | | |
| Put on pajamas | | | | | | | |
| Put clothes in hamper | | | | | | | |
| Pick up toys | | | | | | | |
| Read bedtime story | | | | | | | |

## DAILY CHORES

Each family member should list his or her name next to the chores he or she will take on permanently—either daily, on weekends, or on weekdays.

## DAILY CHORES

| | Mon | Tue | Wed | Thu | Fri | Sat | Sun |
|---|---|---|---|---|---|---|---|
| Wake everyone up | | | | | | | |
| Make beds | | | | | | | |
| Fix breakfast | | | | | | | |
| Wash breakfast dishes/clean kitchen | | | | | | | |
| Get everyone lunch or lunch money | | | | | | | |
| Get children to school or babysitter | | | | | | | |
| Pick up children | | | | | | | |
| Drive children to extracurricular activities | | | | | | | |
| Fix supper or bring home take-out | | | | | | | |
| Wash supper dishes or clean up take-out mess | | | | | | | |
| Vacuum lightly | | | | | | | |
| Take garbage to garbage can | | | | | | | |
| Care for family pets including cleanup | | | | | | | |
| Sweep floors | | | | | | | |
| Talk with children after school and monitor homework | | | | | | | |
| Bathe and dress toddlers | | | | | | | |
| Get clothes ready for next day | | | | | | | |

## WEEKLY CHORES

Each family member should list his or her name next to the chores he or she will take on permanently and do once weekly. You can agree on the day of the week the chore will be done or on a deadline (for example: The chore must be done by Sunday night at 7 p.m.).

| WEEKLY CHORES | PERSON RESPONSIBLE/DEADLINE |
|---|---|
| Upkeep sprinkler system | |
| Mow lawn | |
| Water lawn | |
| Pull weeds | |
| Water plants | |
| Sort clothes | |
| Wash clothes | |
| Put away clothes | |
| Strip beds and wash sheets | |
| Take garbage out | |
| Take garbage can to curb | |
| Iron clothes | |
| Take inventory and shop for new clothes | |
| Polish furniture | |
| Vacuum thoroughly | |
| Sweep wood or tile floors | |
| Mop wood or tile floors | |
| Dust | |
| Clean tub or shower | |
| Clean toilet | |
| Pick up clutter | |
| Plan menu | |
| Buy groceries | |

APPENDIX B — HOUSEHOLDER CHORE LISTS

## PERIODIC CHORES

Each family member should list his or her name next to the chores he or she will take on permanently.

| PERIODIC CHORES | PERSON RESPONSIBLE/DEADLINE |
|---|---|
| Clean ovens | |
| Defrost freezer | |
| Clean out refrigerator | |
| Shampoo carpets | |
| Wash walls and baseboards | |
| Clean cupboards | |
| Clean closets | |
| Wash interior windows | |
| Wash exterior windows | |
| Maintain automobiles internally (engine) | |
| Maintain automobiles externally (cleaning) | |
| Clean garage | |
| Respond to plumbing problems | |

## PERIODIC CHORES, CONTINUED

Each family member should list his or her name next to the chores he or she will take on permanently.

| PERIODIC CHORES | PERSON RESPONSIBLE/DEADLINE |
|---|---|
| Respond to electrical problems | |
| Respond to appliance problems | |
| Maintain heating and cooling systems | |
| Maintain house exterior (paint, gutters, and so on) | |
| Repair roof or arrange for roofer | |
| Do interior construction projects | |
| Do exterior construction projects | |
| Shovel snow | |
| Plant annual flowers | |
| Trim hedges | |
| Maintain soil (fertilize) | |
| Take children to doctor | |
| Take children to dentist | |
| Take children for haircuts | |

## CHORES FOR HOLIDAYS

Each family member should list his or her name next to the chores he or she will take on permanently.

| CHORES FOR HOLIDAYS | PERSON RESPONSIBLE/DEADLINE |
|---|---|
| **Preparation for children's birthdays:** | |
| Buy presents | |
| Buy or make cake | |
| Plan party | |
| Buy groceries | |
| Buy decorations | |
| Send party invitations (or make calls) | |
| Host party | |
| Clean up after party | |
| **Preparation for Thanksgiving:** | |
| Buy groceries | |
| Send invitations (or make calls) | |
| Cook dinner | |
| Cook desserts | |
| Clean up after dinner | |

## CHORES FOR HOLIDAYS AND OTHER SPECIAL EVENTS

| CHORES FOR SPECIAL EVENTS | PERSON RESPONSIBLE/DEADLINE |
|---|---|
| **Preparation for winter holiday:** | |
| String lights (decorate exterior) | |
| Decorate interior | |
| Buy presents | |
| Wrap presents | |
| Send holiday cards | |
| Send invitations (or make calls) | |
| Buy groceries | |
| Cook dinner | |
| Cook desserts (bake cookies) | |
| Arrange for travel | |
| Arrange for hosting guests | |

## CHORES FOR VACATIONS AND WEEKEND GETAWAYS

Each family member should list his or her name next to the chores he or she will take on permanently.

| CHORES FOR VACATIONS AND WEEKEND GETAWAYS | PERSON RESPONSIBLE/DEADLINE |
|---|---|
| Plan the vacation | |
| Make arrangements and reservations | |
| Prepare clothes | |
| Pack suitcases | |
| Pack children's play toys | |
| Get children dressed and out the door | |
| Unpack and wash clothes | |
| Put everything away | |

# PACKING FOR CAMPING (OR OTHER RECREATION)

Each family member should list his or her name next to the chores he or she will take on permanently.

| PACKING FOR CAMPING (OR OTHER RECREATION) | PERSON RESPONSIBLE/DEADLINE |
|---|---|
| Pack gear (list individual items) | |
| Plan menu | |
| Shop for groceries | |
| Pack food | |
| Pack clothes | |
| Prepare camp trailer or vehicle | |

# CHORES WHILE CAMPING (OR OTHER RECREATION)

| CHORES FOR CAMPING (OR OTHER RECREATION) | PERSON RESPONSIBLE/DEADLINE |
|---|---|
| Cook or prepare breakfast | |
| Clean up after breakfast | |
| Cook or prepare lunch | |
| Clean up after lunch | |
| Cook or prepare dinner | |
| Clean up after dinner | |

# CHORES AFTER CAMPING (OR OTHER RECREATION)

| CHORES AFTER CAMPING (OR OTHER RECREATION) | PERSON RESPONSIBLE/DEADLINE |
|---|---|
| Unpack equipment | |
| Unpack clothing | |
| Clean the camp trailer or vehicle | |
| Wash clothing | |
| Put clean clothing away | |
| Clean equipment | |
| Put equipment away | |
| Put food away | |

## CHORES ASSOCIATED WITH BABIES AND TODDLERS

Each family member should list his or her name next to the chores he or she will take on permanently.

| CHORES ASSOCIATED WITH BABIES AND TODDLERS | PERSON RESPONSIBLE/DEADLINE |
| --- | --- |
| Bathe and dress baby in the morning | |
| Bathe baby at night | |
| Change diapers during the day | |
| Change diapers at night | |
| Feed baby during the day | |
| Feed baby at night | |
| Get baby down for daytime naps | |
| Get baby down for bed | |
| Get up at night with baby | |
| Hold and comfort baby when cranky or sick | |
| Take baby to doctor | |
| Hold or keep baby occupied when partner does chore | |

## CHORES FOR MANAGING HOUSEHOLD FINANCES

One adult family member should list his or her name next to the financial chores and take them on permanently. Discuss who does each chore or group of chores best. One person may be responsible for most or all of these chores.

### CHORES FOR MANAGING HOUSEHOLD FINANCES

| Chore | PERSON RESPONSIBLE/DEADLINE |
|---|---|
| Sort and answer mail | |
| Pay bills | |
| Make deposits at the bank | |
| Arrange for gifts or money for weddings, birthdays, bereavement, etc. | |
| Pay for children's school fees | |
| Manage investments | |
| Update partner on money matters | |
| Keep records | |
| Prepare taxes or gather information and delegate to professional | |

Use this blank chart for any other tasks that you need to divide among householders.

**CHORES FOR** _____

**PERSON RESPONSIBLE/DEADLINE**

# APPENDIX C

## A FEW REMINDERS

**T**RY POSTING THESE REMINDERS on an index card, as you would in the "Rule of the Ruler" exercise.

1. Pick your battles. Let the little things pass. This focuses your energy on more important issues.
2. Compromise: It's his house too. If a man's house is his castle, what kind of a castle do you think it would be if he was told on a regular basis how to live in it?
3. Dispel the "me" generation myths:

### Myth #1

If you are not happy in your marriage, it is not healthy for you or your children for you to stay.

If happiness were the standard for judging a marriage, divorce would be justified in the average marriage once a day. If you were happy in the first place, you can get happy again. The key is in discovering specifically what you want and then using a successful program to get it. A marriage counselor is a lot less expensive than a divorce. Don't stay in an unhappy marriage; do whatever it takes to make it happy again.

### Myth #2

It is better for children to see parents in a divorce than to see them fighting all the time.

Chances are, if you're fighting all the time while you're married, you will continue to fight after the divorce. Only then you will be fighting over the children. The children will become the pawns and absorb guilt and resentment.

## Myth #3

It's not healthy for the parents or the children for couples to stay together for the sake of the children.

In the first place, anything parents do for the sake of the children is wonderful! More wonderful still would be not to force a child to be shifted back and forth. Nor to force him to travel out of town because the court says he should. Nor to force stepparents and stepsiblings on him every time a remarriage occurs. Nor to force him into court to solve your problems.

1. Look around and consider truthfully if you would trade your husband's faults for another man's faults. (Too often we compare our own husband's faults with someone else's good qualities.)
2. Use a 3x5 card to record all of your husband's good qualities and keep it with you. Take it out and read it often.
3. Don't blame him: Your husband might be stuck in this phase of infinite childless wisdom, where he thinks he knows exactly how to handle every situation, because he has never experienced full-time parenting and full-time housekeeping. You were there too before your children thrust you into reality.
4. Nobody is perfect, not even us, so before opting out of a marriage, measure his good qualities against his faults. If he has more good qualities than bad, he is a keeper.
5. Include him in every aspect of your marriage and parenting. Do not refer to the kids as "my" kids, the house as "my" house, and the kitchen as "my" kitchen. How can a husband take ownership if your language excludes him?
6. Don't resent your husband for forgetting your birthday, anniversary, and so forth. The reality is, men forget about these things all the time just because they are men.
7. Consider reminding the whole family, in a comical way,

that your birthday (or other anniversary) is next week, then in three days, and finally tomorrow, and see how excited everyone gets to make something happen.

8. Remember that divorce rarely makes people happier.

9. Remember that women have a 45 percent decrease in their standard of living after a divorce.

10. You haven't yet learned how to fix the problem, so the chances of carrying those problems into your next marriage are high. Then, however, you will have stepfamilies added to the equation.

11. Keep the staggering cost of divorce in mind.

12. Don't react too quickly; don't pull the plug on your marriage only to find out later that you dismissed his good qualities.

13. Make sure that being right doesn't get in the way of getting results.

14. Don't take back the chores just because they aren't being done how you would do them. Train your children when they assume responsibility, leave a tip sheet if necessary, and then . . . relax your standards.

15. Be specific and expect results. He does not know what "help me" means. Does it mean help carry in the groceries? Does it mean follow you around and help with everything? Does it mean something in between?

Remember which types of communication don't work:

| ACTION | INSTANT REACTION | CONSEQUENCES |
|---|---|---|
| Angry outbursts | Sympathy (so you won't be mad) or a bigger fight. | Seldom hears the words behind the anger. Nothing about your situation will change. |
| Crying | Guilt for the moment. | No lasting results. "There she goes again." |
| Threats | Falls on deaf ears. | Knows that you won't follow through with your threats, so he doesn't take them—or you—seriously. |
| Running off in a huff (so he will have to do the work) | Anyone can do anything once. | He does it better than you and proves to himself once again you are the one with the problem. |
| Nagging | Does not listen. Resentment builds. | Less likely to do what you ask and will resent you for asking him to do anything. |
| Whining (self-pity) | Turned off. | Turned off. Victimhood is not attractive. |

Remember what communication works:

- Be strong, timely, and empathetic.
- Lose the word "help."
- Be specific and expect results.

# BIBLIOGRAPHY

Allen, Sarah M., and Allen Hawkins. "Maternal Gatekeeping: Mother's Beliefs and Behaviors that Inhibit Greater Father Involvement in Family Work." *Journal of Marriage and the Family*, 61:199–212.

Bird, C. E. "Gender, Household and Psychological Disease: The Impact of the Amount and Division of Housework." *Journal of Health and Social Behavior*, 40:32–45.

Cohen, Alan H. *Why Your Life Sucks, and What You Can Do about It* (San Diego: Jodere Group, 2002).

Coleman, Joshua. *The Lazy Husband* (New York: St. Martins Press, 2005).

Coltrane, Scott. *Family Man: Fatherhood, Housework, and Gender Equality* (New York: Oxford University Press, 1996).

Coltrane, Scott, and Michele Adams. "When Dads Clean House, It Pays Off Big Time" (Analysis of National Survey Data from the Child Development Supplement of the Panel Study of Income Dynamics). University of California, Riverside, 9 June 2003. http://newsroom.ucr.edu/news_item.html?action=page&id=611.

Covey, Stephen R. *The Seven Habits of Highly Effective People* (New York: Fireside, 1989).

# BIBLIOGRAPHY

Deutsch, Francine. *Halving It All: How Equally Shared Parenting Works* (Cambridge, MA: Harvard University Press, 2000).

Doherty, William J. *Take Back Your Marriage: Sticking Together in a World that Pulls Us Apart* (New York: The Guilford Press, 2001).

Dyer, Wayne. *Your Erroneous Zones: Escape Negative Thinking and Take Control of Your Life* (New York: Avon, 2001).

Gottman, John, PhD. *The Seven Principles for Making Marriage Work* (New York: Three Rivers Press, 1999).

———. *Why Marriages Succeed or Fail, And How You Can Make Yours Last* (New York: Fireside, 1994).

Haltzman, Scott, M.D. *The Secrets of Happily Married Men* (San Francisco: Jossey Bass, 2006).

Hochschild, Arlie R. *The Second Shift: Working Parents and the Revolution at Home* (New York: Viking-Penguin, 1989).

Huber, Joan, and Glenna Spitze. *Sex Stratification: Children, Housework, and Jobs* (New York: Academic Press, 1983). Cited in Hochschild, 1989.

Katie, Byron and Stephen Mitchell. *Loving What Is: Four Questions That Can Change Your Life* (New York: Three Rivers Press, 2003).

Leman, Kevin, PhD. *Women Who Try Too Hard: Breaking the Pleaser Habits* (Grand Rapids, MI: Fleming H. Revell Company, 1998).

McGraw, Phillip C., PhD. *Life Strategies: Doing What Works, Doing What Matters* (New York: Hyperion, 1999).

Peale, Norman Vincent. *The Power of Positive Thinking* (Rawlings, NY: Foundation for Christian Living, 1978).

Rousell, Michael A. *Sudden Influence: How Spontaneous Events Shape Our Lives* (Westport, CT: Praeger Publishers, 2007).

Wilson, Sandra D., PhD. *Shame-Free Parenting* (Downers Grove, IL: InterVarsity Press, 1992).

# ABOUT THE AUTHOR

**SHERRI MILLS** is still in her first marriage of forty-two years with a loving husband who shares the household workload and three loving children, now grown with children of their own.

She considers her forty-plus years as a hairdresser her "research on life." She has listened to real-life family problems and followed real-life outcomes—successes and failures—and through several generations, longer and more extensively than marriage counselors can.

When Sherri solved her own marital burnout from trying to "do it all" as full-time wife, mother, housekeeper, and breadwinner, she thought all modern couples would soon find their own way to equitably share householder work. Instead, year after year, she continued to hear from women who were angry, frustrated, and ready to divorce husbands who "won't help." Their pain prompted her to write this book.

You can contact Sherri at sher@emerytelcom.net or look her up at sherrimillsauthor.com and nomoredivorces.blogspot.com.